E-Mail Etiquette
for Business Professionals

ALSO FROM SYNTAXIS PRESS

A Grammar Guide for Business Professionals
Presentation Skills for Business Professionals
A Writing Guide for Business Professionals

E-Mail Etiquette
for Business Professionals

■ by Ellen Jovin

SYNTAXIS PRESS • NEW YORK

Published by Syntaxis Press™, a division of Syntaxis, Inc.
2109 Broadway, Suite 12-104
New York, New York 10023
www.syntaxis.com
info@syntaxis.com
(212) 799-3000

ISBN: 978-0-9785823-3-3
Library of Congress Control Number: 2006911328

Text set in Scala and Scala Sans
Design by Alton Creative, Inc.
Printed in the United States of America

9   8   7   6   5   4   3

Contents

Preface ix

Introduction: Communicating in
an Electronic Age 1

Chapter 1. The Nature of E-Mail 5

Chapter 2. Anatomy of an E-Mail Message 11
2.1 *To* and *From* Fields 12
2.2 Subject Lines 13
2.3 Body 14
    2.3.1 Salutations 15
    2.3.2 Recipient Names 21
    2.3.3 Message Content 22
    2.3.4 Closings 23
    2.3.5 Signature Files 27
    2.3.6 Font 33

Chapter 3. Minding the Details 35
3.1 Capitalization 35
3.2 Punctuation 36
    3.2.1 Exclamation Points 37
    3.2.2 Ellipses and Dashes 38
    3.2.3 Aggressive Punctuation!! 39
3.3 Spelling 40
3.4 Abbreviations and Emoticons 40
3.5 Responding to Careless E-Mailers 41

Chapter 4. Organization Matters 45

4.1   Get to the Point Quickly 45

4.2   Paragraph Length 48

4.3   Order of Ideas 49

4.4   Development 54

4.5   Bulleting 55

4.6   Long E-Mail Messages 56

4.7   Conclusions 57

Chapter 5. Editing Your E-Mail 59

5.1   Sentence Structure 60

       5.1.1   Sentence Variety 60

       5.1.2   The Dreaded Comma Splice 63

       5.1.3   Passive Voice 64

5.2   Word Choice 69

       5.2.1   Vague Language 69

       5.2.2   Wordiness and Ornate Language 70

       5.2.3   Too Few Words 72

       5.2.4   Trite Language 74

5.3   Editing Techniques 75

       5.3.1   Printing and Proofreading 76

       5.3.2   Reading Aloud 76

       5.3.3   Spell-Checkers 76

       5.3.4   Editing Partners 78

       5.3.5   Breaks 78

Chapter 6. Relationship Management 81

Chapter 7. Special Topics 87

7.1   Automatic Replies 87

7.2   Copying 92

7.3	Blind Copying	92
7.4	Forwarding	94
	7.4.1 When Not to Forward	95
	7.4.2 Making Your Messages Forwardable	97
7.5	Managing E-Mail Dialogues	101
7.6	Attachments	102
7.7	Handheld Devices	103
7.8	E-Mail Templates	104
7.9	Urgent E-Mail	105
7.10	Read Receipts	106
7.11	Meeting Etiquette	106

Chapter 8. Reducing E-Mail Volume 109

Chapter 9. Reader Responsibilities 115

Conclusion 121

Index 125

Preface

Words are the currency of virtually every business transaction. Words persuade. They educate. They clarify needs and intentions. Words inspire.

Nonetheless, many business professionals don't often stop to consider whether they are using words to their greatest advantage. The consequence: every day in every industry, organizational effectiveness is diminished by dull presentations, inappropriate or ungrammatical e-mail, and wordy, jargon-laden memos and reports. This book is one of a series of Syntaxis guides designed to combat problems such as these by developing oral and written communication skills needed in the workplace.

The advice offered in this series grew out of our experience training employees of leading firms in diverse industries. Based in New York City, Syntaxis conducts seminars in presentation skills, business writing, grammar, and e-mail etiquette throughout North America. The firm also provides one-on-one presentation skills coaching for senior executives.

These communication skills books are distributed to participants in Syntaxis training sessions, but they were designed to be standalone guides as well, for any professional who would like to speak and write more powerfully.

Ellen Jovin Brandt Johnson
Principal, Syntaxis *Principal, Syntaxis*

Introduction

Communicating in an Electronic Age

THE ADVENT OF ELECTRONIC MAIL has expedited business communications — but at a great cost to clarity and basic business etiquette. Many electronic messages reach their destinations in a state of linguistic chaos, lacking the traditional hallmarks of good business correspondence: a clear purpose, logical organization, and appropriate punctuation and mechanics.

Despite the conversational feel of much computer-based communication, e-mail is a written form and should therefore observe many of the conventions associated with traditional business letters and memos. This book considers these conventions while also addressing issues new to a world of increasingly electronic interactions — for example, copying, forwarding, and other technological capabilities.

Although it is often treated as conversation, e-mail is not conversation, and people who use e-mail for business communications must always remember: e-mail endures. Unethical or inappropriate e-mail messages can do significant damage not only to the sender's reputation, but also to the reputation (and perhaps balance sheet) of the sender's employer. Used wisely, though, e-mail can be a powerful, efficient communications tool to inform, influence, inspire — and, ultimately, to advance one's career. The goal of this book is to help e-mailers realize the full potential of their electronic business communications.

There are certain e-mail topics this book does not cover. For example, it does not address technical aspects of e-mailing, such as choosing between HTML and plain text, nor does it cover e-mail marketing strategies. Also, keep in mind that the following discussion concerns professional e-mail habits, not personal ones (though quite a few parents and grandparents would be pleased to see recommendations from this book implemented in the e-mail messages they receive from their younger relatives!).

This book is not intended to replace or override your company's specific policies on e-mail use. Heed your employer's e-mail requirements and guidelines, and be sensitive to your unique organizational environment, as e-mail culture can vary from one company to the next.

Chapter 1
The Nature of E-Mail

Before the age of e-mail, memos and business letters dominated the world of business correspondence. Memos were used for internal communication with other employees of one's firm, while letters typically went to clients, vendors, and others outside the firm. Memos were often mass-printed (or mass-copied), and perhaps mass-stapled, after which an employee, or multiple employees, would place them one at a time into recipients' mailboxes. Letters were printed, put in envelopes, sealed, stamped, and delivered by the U.S. Postal Service. Both memos and letters may have had attachments in the form of reports or other documents.

Today a third category of business correspondence—e-mail—has encroached on the traditional turf of memos and letters. At the same time, it has introduced a new type of correspondence that blends elements of both spoken and written communication styles. Figure 1 on the next page illustrates the current correspondence landscape.

Suppose you e-mail a client about a new product your company has just introduced. That e-mail

Figure 1 • Business Correspondence in the Age of E-Mail

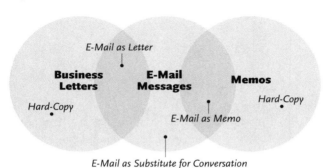

could be considered an approximate electronic substitute for a letter. After all, if the year were 1993, you might mail that client a printed letter containing the same information. Even today, you might do that if you wanted to have a particular aesthetic effect. Nice letterhead with a strong corporate logo has an impact difficult to replicate in e-mail.

While hard-copy memos are rare today, their electronic equivalent is not: many e-mails go out that are virtually identical to the traditional memo. Both types of correspondence have *To* and *From* fields, a date, and a subject line. The only noteworthy difference is that the e-mail versions aren't printed out for distribution.

A third type of e-mail acts as a substitute for what would historically have been an oral communication, whether over the phone or in person. These e-mails tend to be more informal, but they should still be professional.

The problem is, they often aren't.

Consider this scenario. In the mid-1990s, if a manager had wanted a document from an employee, he or she might have phoned. The conversation would perhaps have sounded something like this:

Employee: Hello?

Manager: Hi, John. How are you?

Employee: Fine, Janet. How are you?

Manager: Great. I was wondering whether you had a copy of the latest user guide.

Employee: Absolutely. Would you like me to bring it over?

Manager: Yeah, that would be great. Thank you.

Employee: Sure. See you in a minute.

The words themselves would certainly have conveyed information, but our hypothetical employee, John, would have gleaned additional information from the manager's tone of voice. He would have been able to make reasonable guesses about whether she was in a good mood, pleased with his work, in a hurry, and so on.

Such an exchange might alternatively have

taken place in person, in which case John would also have received visual cues through Janet's facial expressions and body language.

Today such an interaction is increasingly likely to take place through e-mail. When a person sends an e-mail, however, vocal and physical cues are absent. Without accompanying nonverbal signals, messages can easily come across as rude, or curt, or confusing—despite the good intentions of the sender. Therefore, the details of an e-mail matter. It is by paying attention to those details that the writer helps ensure that an outgoing e-mail accomplishes its mission.

Chapter 2

Anatomy of an E-Mail Message

E-MAIL PROFESSIONALISM requires an understanding of an e-mail's various components. Figure 2 illustrates these components, which are discussed in detail in this chapter.

Figure 2 • ANATOMY OF AN E-MAIL

2.1 *To* and *From* Fields

In the *To* field of most e-mail messages, you will find two elements: the recipient's name and e-mail address, as illustrated below:

To: John Smith <john.smith@xyz-inc.com>

Sometimes e-mail addresses display without the name, though:

To: <john.smith@xyz-inc.com>

If the name isn't displaying automatically, use your e-mail software to add it. If you don't know how, ask a technologically adept person to help you. Why bother? Including the person's name has a friendlier appearance than the more technical-looking e-mail address by itself.

By the way, you should also make sure that when you send out messages, your own e-mail address is accompanied by your full name in the *From* field. If you like to include a middle initial with your name, don't forget the period after the initial. For example:

From: Joanna A. Rogers <joanna.rogers@xyz-inc.com>

Additional comments on names appear throughout this chapter.

2.2 **Subject Lines**

The subject line of an e-mail should be brief yet descriptive. After all, it is by scanning subject lines that many people will find your message among a slew of other incoming messages competing for their attention.

Suppose you send two colleagues an e-mail with an attached copy of a report about technology expenses for the second quarter of 2007. Simply writing *Technology Report* in the subject line is not enough to tell them what the topic of your message is. And *Report on technology expenses for the second quarter of 2007 attached* is long and meandering. If your subject contains too many words, it will be more difficult for recipients to read it quickly, and it is also possible that their e-mail software will truncate the subject so that they can't see all the information.

Consider the following alternative:

Subject: Technology Expense Report Q2 2007

This version is superior to the previous two options because it is both concise and precise. The reader will quickly understand exactly what he or she is receiving.

Regarding capitalization of your subject line, you have multiple choices. Naturally you should always capitalize proper nouns such as *Joan* or *Empire State Building*, but for the rest of the words in your subject you can choose between the following options:

■ Capitalize the subject line as you would a title, beginning everything except minor words with capital letters.

■ Capitalize the first word of the subject, as well as any proper nouns, but begin any other words with lower-case letters.

The decision is a stylistic and aesthetic one, based on your own preferences and the context. Capitalizing the subject line like a title often gives it a more polished, professional appearance. For long subject lines, however, initial capital letters throughout can at times be a bit overwhelming; in such cases, sometimes a better choice is to use initial caps for just the first word and any proper nouns.

Subjects with no capital letters at all generally don't look as polished as the two options described above.

2.3 **Body**

In an e-mail, the term *body* typically refers to everything that appears in the freeform box, including the salutation, signature file (i.e., the sender's contact information), and all the content in between.

This use of *body* should not be confused with the way the term is used in discussions of document structure. See Chapter 4 for a discussion of *body* in the traditional document-structure sense.

2.3.1 *Salutations*

The salutation is the opening line of your e-mail where you address the recipient directly, usually by name. In business letters, your choices for salutations are limited to phrases such as:

Dear Ms. Smith:

Dear Max:

To Whom It May Concern:

In the world of e-mail, however, a number of salutation styles are acceptable. Which one is best for a given situation depends on factors such as your relationship to the recipient, the culture of your firm or department, and the content and context of the message. In addition, salutations for a single recipient generally differ from those for multiple recipients.

Although recipient information appears in the *To* field, for most professional e-mails you should still greet the person in the body of the message. A greeting adds warmth that a name and e-mail address in the remote *To* field do not. In ongoing dialogues, you may consider deleting the greeting after the initial exchange, but if you are writing to clients or to people at your firm who are senior to you, don't delete the salutation until they begin doing so themselves.

Listed below are various salutations commonly found in e-mail messages directed to a single recipient. Their inclusion here does not necessarily mean they are broadly acceptable; there are comments elaborating on the relevance and appropriateness of each greeting for business e-mail. The salutations are loosely organized from more formal to less formal.

E-MAIL SALUTATIONS FOR A SINGLE RECIPIENT

Salutation	Comments
To Whom It May Concern:	Although this formulation sounds rather old-fashioned and stuffy, it has long had a place in business letters to unknown recipients. A very formal greeting, it could be appropriate in cases such as an e-mailed inquiry regarding a potential vendor's services or an e-mailed complaint.
Dear Sir or Madam:	This option is similar to the one above.
Dear Mr. Smith:	This formal salutation is appropriate when you are e-mailing a person you do not know well or at all—for example, a prospective [Continued]

	client. Depending on your corporate culture, you may also want to use it when writing to someone in your firm who is quite senior to you, particularly if you don't know the person.
Dear James:	Some people find *Dear* along with a first name to be a strange opening for an e-mail, complaining that it feels either too inti-mate—like a personal letter—or too formal. If you aren't comfortable using *Dear* with co-workers, there are certainly other options, but the salutation *Dear* has a long and happy history in business correspondence. Even if you do not use it much internally at your firm, it has a legitimate place in your e-mail reper-toire, particularly for external, international, and formal communications.
James, *James -*	Fine in many contexts. Occasionally the name by itself can sound a little abrupt, but it is a solid opening for many types of e-mail messages.
Good morning, James.	This salutation can be a useful way to begin e-mail messages as it is both businesslike and friendly. Of course, at the time you send the message, it should actually *be* morning in the recipient's time zone.
Hello, James. *Hello, James -*	These salutations may be acceptable for use in a business context with someone you know reasonably well. The punctuation in the second instance is untraditional outside the world of e-mail, but is clear and practical for electronic use.

E-Mail Salutations for a Single Recipient, *Cont'd*

Hello James,	This salutation is common but is punctuated untraditionally and is therefore not an ideal way to begin an e-mail. (According to standard punctuation rules, the greeting requires a comma between *Hello* and *James*, but then the writer would end up with two commas in a two-word salutation, which looks odd.)
Hi, James. *Hi, James -*	For use in a business context, these salutations are usually too casual. *Hi* is a word better reserved for correspondence with friends. However, depending on your corporate culture, these salutations may be acceptable for communications with co-workers you know well.
Hi James,	This salutation is very casual and is also punctuated untraditionally. A comma is needed between *Hi* and *James*, but then the salutation will contain two commas in a row, which looks odd. Although this salutation is common, in business e-mail it may be perceived as unprofessional.

As you can see, it isn't easy to figure out how to address an individual. Addressing a group of people through e-mail can pose an even more formidable challenge. To formulate a salutation for multiple people, consider the composition of the group you will be addressing. If you are writing to your co-workers in the marketing department, for example, you could perhaps begin your message with one of the following salutations:

Dear Colleagues:

Dear Marketing Colleagues:

The appropriateness of these salutations, however, depends on the context. Below are comments on various salutations, some good and some not so good, that appear in group e-mail messages.

E-MAIL SALUTATIONS FOR MULTIPLE RECIPIENTS

Salutation	Comments
Greetings.	Any of these salutations can be used in e-mail going to multiple recipients. In addition, *Greetings* can act as a salutation in an automatic reply you might set up when you are going to be out of the office.
Good morning.	
Good afternoon.	
Dear Sirs:	In a working world populated by both women and men, these salutations are out of date in almost all cases. Theoretically they could still be used with relative safety in a context where every recipient was male, but even in those cases, the formulations would be likely to come across as old-fashioned.
Dear Gentlemen:	
Dear Colleagues:	This salutation is both respectful and friendly. It can be used to address the people in your department or division, assuming that you [*Continued*]

E-MAIL SALUTATIONS FOR MULTIPLE RECIPIENTS, *Cont'd*

	have a good working relationship with them and that the members of the group are of similar professional status or junior to you. Do not, however, use this salutation with a group containing people senior to you.
Jane and Tim, *Dear Jane and Tim:* *Good morning, Jane and Tim.*	If you are addressing two people, you may use their names in combination with various greetings from the table of e-mail salutations for individual recipients. Some common options appear to the left. For e-mails going to more than two people, it can sound awkward to refer to all of them by name.
[None]	Many people don't like to receive e-mails without salutations. Nonetheless, if your corporate culture supports it, sending a mass e-mail with no greeting at all can make sense. Such an e-mail is, after all, virtually identical in form to the traditional memo, which does not contain a greeting.
Hello,	If you can't figure out a way to address your recipients directly, whether as *Marketing Staff*, *Colleagues*, or something else, the first three salutations in this table (*Greetings*, *Good morning*, or *Good afternoon*) may be preferable to the more casual, less professional-sounding *Hello*.
Hi, all! *Hi, all.* *Hi!*	Unless you have a very casual working environment—and even if you do—these formulations can sometimes be perceived as unprofessional. Proceed with caution.

Guys,	Like *Dear Sirs* and *Dear Gentlemen*, this salutation may offend female recipients. In addition, it is too casual for most workplace correspondence.

2.3.2 *Recipient Names*

It is critical to get people's names right in e-mail salutations (for example, *Dear Ms. Smith* or *Good morning, John*). Below are some guidelines and cautionary notes about name etiquette in e-mail.

- **Spelling.** Spell the recipient's name correctly. Triple-check unusual and unfamiliar names.

- **Form of first name.** If you are addressing a person by first name, use the correct form of that name. Even if the person's name happens to be a name that is often shortened, such as *Michael*, don't automatically assume that that individual is in the habit of shortening it. Use *Michael* unless you come across concrete evidence that the person uses *Mike*. That evidence may come from sources such as the bottom of an e-mail from him — if he signs off as *Mike* — or a voicemail message from him starting off, "Hi, this is Mike." Once you learn that the recipient prefers the shortened form, you should use that version of the name.

- **Initials.** Don't address a person by his or her initials, unless you have specifically been told — by a reliable source!—that initials are how that person prefers to be addressed.

- **Mr. and Ms.** When you address people by their surnames in a business setting, use *Mr.* for men and *Ms.* for women. If a woman specifically requests that you address her with *Mrs.* or *Miss*, however, you should honor her request.

- **Unknown gender.** It is a challenge to send a formal e-mail to a person whose gender you can't determine from the name. How do you know whether to use *Mr.* or *Ms.*? Fortunately, you are not without recourse. First, you can call the general number for the person's company and ask the operator whether the person is male or female. If for some reason that isn't an option, try searching for the name on the Internet to see whether you can glean anything about the likely gender. If you immediately find a dozen men with that name, and no women, then you can probably assume your recipient is a man. Finally, if you are still unsure, you can as a last resort use the first and last name together, without a *Mr.* or *Ms.*—*Dear Pat Lee*, for example. This option is stylistically awkward, but is probably better than guessing. If you think a less formal greeting is appropriate, you can of course avoid the issue by writing *Dear Pat* instead.

2.3.3 Message Content

Most e-mail messages are no longer than a few paragraphs, and many messages are much shorter — a mere line or two. There is no minimum length requirement, but an e-mail should always be clear. Please see Chapter 4, "Organization Matters," for comments on long e-mails.

In most e-mail messages, you should skip a line after your salutation, between each paragraph, and before your closing (e.g., *Regards*). It is not necessary to indent at the beginning of each paragraph; skipping a line between paragraphs is sufficient. See Figure 2, page 11, for an illustration of appropriate e-mail spacing.

One cautionary note: if you are writing to someone who usually reads e-mail on a BlackBerry or similar device, you may want to make adjustments to this format. See Section 7.7 for additional discussion of e-mailing considerations for handheld devices.

2.3.4 *Closings*

There are multiple ways to close e-mail messages. First you must choose your closing word or phrase, if you wish to include one — for example, *Thank you* or *Regards*. If you know your recipient and are addressing him or her by first name, in most cases you can then add just your first name. If you are writing more formally and are addressing the recipient by last name, it is usually preferable to close your e-mail with your full name.

Figure 3 shows a closing, accompanied by the signature file (which is covered in detail in the next section), for an e-mail from a person who knows his recipient fairly well.

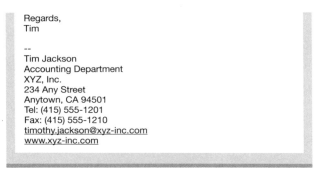

```
Regards,
Tim

--
Tim Jackson
Accounting Department
XYZ, Inc.
234 Any Street
Anytown, CA 94501
Tel: (415) 555-1201
Fax: (415) 555-1210
timothy.jackson@xyz-inc.com
www.xyz-inc.com
```

Figure 3 • Closing Format, Less Formal E-Mail

His closing word (*Regards*) and name appear on consecutive lines.

If he were sending a message to a potential client, though, he might sign his message as follows:

```
Sincerely,

Tim Jackson
Accounting Department
XYZ, Inc.
234 Any Street
Anytown, CA 94501
Tel: (415) 555-1201
Fax: (415) 555-1210
timothy.jackson@xyz-inc.com
www.xyz-inc.com
```

Figure 4 • Closing Format, Formal E-Mail

In Figures 3 and 4, the font used in the e-mail body is the same as the signature file font. If, however, your signature file has been specially formatted (preferably by your art department or a professional designer) so that its appearance is distinct from the rest of the text in the body of your message, you should in a formal e-mail repeat your full name after your closing, as shown in Figure 5. Otherwise it may seem as though you didn't bother to "sign" your e-mail.

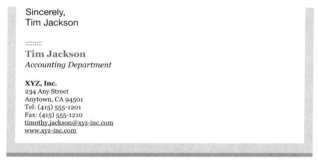

Figure 5 • ALTERNATIVE CLOSING FORMAT, FORMAL E-MAIL

Some businesspeople put periods after their names in closings. If you feel the temptation to do so, resist it.

Incorrect	Correct
Regards,	Regards,
Tim.	Tim

In more casual e-mails, it may be fine to sign off without a closing phrase and just put your name.

As a general rule, though, don't sign off with just your initials. If you use initials, you risk irritating recipients who may view this shorthand as a sign that they are not worth the time it would take to write your actual name. (Remember a cardinal rule of e-mailing: people who are bothered by your habits won't necessarily tell you how they feel.) Some people don't care, of course, and if you use e-mail shorthand with your long-time colleague who sits two desks away, that may be fine.

Below are some common e-mail closings accompanied by comments on their use.

E-Mail Closings

Closing Phrase	Comments
Sincerely,	This is a polite, professional way to close, but is most appropriate for formal e-mails, such as initial communications with prospective clients. In e-mails with people you already know, Sincerely may come across as excessively formal.
Regards,	This is a safe, acceptable closing term in almost all situations, ranging from fairly casual to quite formal.
Thank you,	This closing is ideal when you want to show appreciation for something the recipient has done or is going to do for you. (If you want to be very appreciative and say Thank you [Continued]

	very much, then you can keep that as a separate sentence and perhaps add a different closing. For instance:
	Thank you very much.
	Regards, Rose
Thanks,	Similar to *Thank you* above, but more casual. Most appropriate if you are writing to co-workers you know well and have a good relationship with, or when you are e-mailing, say, vendors or people who are somewhat junior to you. If you have reason to be really appreciative, *Thank you* is generally a better choice.
[None]	For quick, casual e-mails to people with whom you have an established business relationship, closing with just your first name is a common and acceptable practice.
Best,	Ending with *Best* may give the impression that the e-mail writer was simply too busy to bother completing the closing. Best *what*, after all? It could perhaps be considered the e-mail equivalent of a host's failing to see a guest all the way to the door at the end of a dinner party.

2.3.5 *Signature Files*

In your e-mail software, there should be an option that enables you to create a signature file — in other words, a block of contact information that appears automatically at the bottom of all of your outgoing messages. Although you have a number of aesthetic alternatives, a standard signature file might look something like this:

```
Renée Jones
Director, Training
XYZ, Inc.
123 Anywhere Street
New York, NY 10024
Tel: (212) 555-0469
Fax: (212) 555-1472
renee.jones@xyz-inc.com
www.xyz-inc.com
```

Figure 6 • SAMPLE SIGNATURE FILE, EXTERNAL COMMUNICATIONS

Why is a signature file necessary? For one thing, it helps an e-mail appear polished and professional; it is like stationery for electronic messages. In addition, if recipients of a message don't know you very well, the absence of a signature file can cause confusion as they try to figure out who you are. Finally, you should generally make it as easy as possible for recipients to find you; by including contact information in your standard communications, you enable them to reach you with minimal effort.

Your e-mail software may well allow you to set up a shorter, alternative signature file for internal communications with employees of your firm. Suppose, for example, that Renée Jones from the signature file above is e-mailing someone in her company's accounting department. An appropriate signature file for internal use could be:

Renée Jones
Director, Training
Tel: (212) 555-0469
Fax: (212) 555-1472

Figure 7 • Sample Signature File, Internal Communications

Of course, not every e-mail should have a signature file. Sometimes you may not want people to have your contact information. For example, if you are sending a message asking someone to stop sending you unsolicited e-mail, consider deleting the signature file so that you don't give the person even more information than he or she already has.

In addition, if you are having an ongoing e-mail dialogue with someone, it is often better — after your initial exchange — to omit the signature file in subsequent messages that accumulate within the same e-mail chain. That way your contact information won't show up repeatedly within the growing pile of messages.

There are multiple ways to order your contact information. Usually the sender's name, title, department, company name, and street address appear first, but after that, you have multiple options.

If you like, for example, you can then put phone number, fax number, e-mail address, and website. Or you could put website, e-mail, phone, then fax. Whatever order you choose, it should have an internal logic, and you should carefully proof-read every letter and punctuation mark for errors and inconsistencies. In the signature file examples on the previous pages, *Tel:* doesn't include a period even though *Tel* is an abbreviation, but you could also write *Tel.:* if you prefer. The reason for omitting the period would be purely aesthetic, to make it a closer visual partner for *Fax*.

Many signature files are far from polished. They may suffer from flaws ranging from inconsistent formatting to editing errors. Here are some things to check for in your own:

- Is the font consistent?

- Do you use colors? Unless you are a professional designer or are receiving advice from one, stick to black, as erratic color can make your e-mail message appear unprofessional and distract from the content of your message.

- Do you include your business title and department below your name? If your firm doesn't use titles, just put the department.

- Do you include your physical address and all relevant details, such as suite, room, or floor? If you can't or don't want to include your address, that may be fine, but make sure you have a good reason.

- Is your use of abbreviations consistent and

appropriate? You can afford to be sparing with abbreviations in your signature file, especially less familiar ones such as *Fl.* for *Floor* or *Ste.* for *Suite*. It's not as though you have to retype the words each time, so where you think it looks better, spell out the word.

- Do you include your company's website address? If not, consider adding it.

- Do you include your telephone and fax numbers, complete with area codes, in a neat, consistent format? Among the various options are:

(212) 555-0989
212-555-0989
212.555.0989

- Do you include a cell phone number? Do not do so unless (1) you check your messages regularly, (2) you have a professional outgoing greeting, and (3) you are prepared to answer your cell phone in a professional manner, as you might when sitting at your desk. If it is your personal cell phone and you use it primarily for personal calls, you should probably not include your cell number in the signature file. It is generally unprofessional to take a work-related call in a crowded bar.

You can present the cell number in various ways, including:

Cell: (917) 555-1987
Mobile: 917-555-1987

Normally the cell number would appear after your office number and before the fax, but if your cell phone is the primary way people reach you, you might consider listing it before the office number.

■ Do you include your e-mail address? Although this information is available in the *From* field, it is helpful to include it in your signature file so that e-mail recipients can quickly cut and paste all of your contact data into their records. Keep in mind that not all recipients use the same e-mail software you do, so even if it takes only a mouse click to add a new contact to your software, the process in theirs might be more complicated. Also, make sure your e-mail address doesn't contain a typographical error—one of the worst typos you can have! (Suppose an important client uses that address to e-mail you and the message is returned undeliverable. Very embarrassing to you, and very annoying to the client.)

■ Are there any other typos or misspellings?

■ Is the spacing consistent? Do you have any extra or missing spaces between words or around punctuation?

■ Is your capitalization consistent?

■ Do you include favorite personal quotes or sayings? If so, delete them. A business e-mail is not an opportunity to communicate irrelevant information about your own interests or personal philosophy. It may, however, provide an opportunity to promote your firm. If your company has a marketing tag line, it may be appropriate and perhaps even desirable to include it, as long as you have corporate approval.

- Is the information complete?

2.3.6 *Font*

Avoid unusual or eccentric fonts in business e-mail. The font should generally be black, and neither too big nor too small. Arial, often 10-point, is a common default font for e-mail; it has a clean appearance and is easy to read. Other options include (but are not limited to) Verdana and Tahoma. Justifiable exceptions to these font guidelines might be found in a professionally designed signature file, created under the guidance of a corporate art department or designer. It is fine, though, to use the same font for your signature file that you use throughout the body of your e-mail.

If you wish to depart from these recommendations for a particular type of e-mail—a marketing message, for instance—seek the design advice of a qualified professional.

Chapter 3
Minding the Details

Minding the details of e-mail—capitalization, punctuation, and so on—shows respect for the reader's time. Most people find it easier and more pleasant to read a carefully edited e-mail with appropriate capitalization and punctuation than they do an all-lower-case, punctuation-free message. If you disregard such details, you will distract from your content.

You also risk giving the impression that the recipient's convenience is less important than your time—the small amount of time it would take to fix these minor problems.

3.1 **Capitalization**

Before you dispense with traditional capitalization, consider the reasons that capital letters exist. First, capital letters provide important information to the reader. When you capitalize a word, you indicate something about it. Perhaps it is the first word in a sentence; perhaps it is a proper noun such as *John* or *Pepsi*. In a business environment, where you want to convey the maximum amount of information in the minimum amount of time, standard capitalization can help ensure clarity in your writing.

Therefore, don't underuse capital letters. It is especially risky to write people's names in all lower-case letters, a practice that some could perceive as insulting. Particularly if you are writing to a person senior to you, use standard initial caps for his or her name, even if the person habitually lower-cases yours. The same goes for clients.

Don't use all capital letters, either. Writing e-mails entirely in capital letters is widely perceived as the electronic equivalent of shouting. Many readers find this habit extremely irksome; heed your audience's preferences.

3.2 **Punctuation**

Like capitalization, punctuation carries meaning. Commas, periods, semicolons, and other marks indicate boundaries and relationships between ideas. If you leave out punctuation, the act of reading your e-mail messages automatically becomes more difficult for recipients, who must figure out those boundaries and relationships for themselves. Courteous correspondents take care to make their readers as comfortable as possible; in doing so, they also ensure that greater attention is paid to the content itself.

Problems with punctuation extend beyond neglect of traditional punctuation to excessive use of certain types of punctuation. In business e-mail, exclamation points, dashes, and ellipses have proliferated beyond the bounds of appropriateness. Below are some cautionary notes on each.

3.2.1 *Exclamation Points*

In our electronic age, exclamation points have become very popular pieces of punctuation. They tend to be far more numerous in e-mail than in any other business documents. That is hardly surprising, as many people e-mail in a conversational mode; exclamation points are a way to show enthusiasm for their subject. Unfortunately, an e-mail message full of exclamation points may come across as unprofessional, or sound as though it is coming from someone young and inexperienced. It is best to use them sparingly.

An example of an appropriate context for an exclamation point might be an encouraging e-mail to someone who works with or for you. For example, it is fine to write something like the following:

You did a wonderful job on the background research!

See Section 3.2.3 ("Aggressive Punctuation!!") for additional comments on the exclamation point.

3.2.2 *Ellipses and Dashes*

In business e-mail, the ellipsis (...) and dash are often used in nonstandard ways. One cause of their popularity is growing uncertainty about standard punctuation rules. Confronted with a pause they are unsure how to punctuate, many e-mailers gravitate towards the seemingly all-purpose ellipsis or dash.

The ellipsis and dash are not all-purpose punctuation, though; they have particular applications. For professional e-mail, you should use them as they are meant to be used. Generally that means the ellipsis won't show up much, as its primary purpose is to indicate missing words, as in quoted material. In more casual e-mail, it is sometimes used to indicate a kind of auditory break, or hesitation, or a sense that something is being continued (*Joe definitely won't attend...it wouldn't be productive*), but these applications should be confined primarily to personal or informal e-mail.

The dash is a relatively flexible piece of punctuation, but distribute your dashes with care! One reason to use a dash is for dramatic emphasis:

> The storm damaged their truck, destroyed their store, and ruined much of their merchandise—but it could not diminish their entrepreneurial enthusiasm.

The dash can also set off parenthetical words

and help ensure clarity. The following sentence could benefit from a pair of dashes.

Confusing

Her colleague, a former teacher, and her sister attended the awards ceremony.

How many people attended the ceremony? It could be two, if the colleague is interpreted to be the former teacher, or it could be three, if the colleague and the former teacher are two different people. If they are not, though, a pair of dashes can resolve the confusion.

Clear

Her colleague—a former teacher—and her sister attended the awards ceremony.

3.2.3 *Aggressive Punctuation!!*

Punctuation is sometimes used as a kind of weapon. Perhaps you yourself have been the victim of a punctuation assault, as in the following examples:

Where is the document I requested??

I asked you to get here by 4:00!!!

When are you going to deliver the folders?!

In general, avoid what could be called *aggressive punctuation*: the combination of multiple consecutive exclamation points and/or question marks (instead of the usual allotment of one) to demonstrate anger, irritation, or urgency. In business communications, such punctuation can be inflammatory or offensive. If you need a document right away, use authoritative but professional language to request it. Don't rely on punctuation to do your dirty work.

3.3 **Spelling**

Professionals are judged on their spelling. Fair or unfair, one of the quickest ways to cause readers to draw negative conclusions about your larger competence is to misspell words.

Fortunately, professionals today have multiple tools — electronic spell-checkers, for example — at their disposal to ensure that messages don't go out with spelling mistakes. Take advantage of them; the benefits far outweigh the time cost. See Chapter 5, "Editing Your E-Mail," for additional comments on editing.

3.4 **Abbreviations and Emoticons**

Some members of the workforce favor a kind of e-mail shorthand common also in instant messages, online chat, and cell phone text messages. Resist the temptation to incorporate such shorthand into work-related e-mail messages.

For example, *lol* stands for "laugh out loud." If you must use it (the act of laughing typically involves sound, so the utility of mentioning that it is out loud is unclear), save it for personal communications. Other shorthand examples you should avoid in professional e-mail messages include:

Thx.
When r u going to arrive?
c u there.

In addition, emoticons such as :-) or :-(are best confined to personal e-mail.

3.5 **Responding to Careless E-Mailers**

What should you do if someone—your supervisor, for instance—habitually sends you messages full of nonstandard capitalization and punctuation? Is it rude not to respond in kind? Could that perhaps seem like an implied criticism of the supervisor's e-mail style?

Not at all, in fact. When you are communicating in writing with someone you work for, it is especially important that you make the experience of reading your message as easy as possible. That doesn't mean you have to adopt an artificially formal style. A simple message such as the one in Figure 8 on the next page could be appropriate.

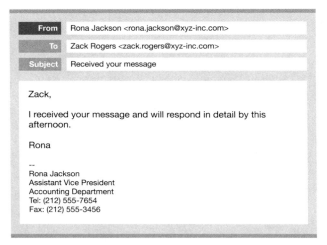

From	Rona Jackson <rona.jackson@xyz-inc.com>
To	Zack Rogers <zack.rogers@xyz-inc.com>
Subject	Received your message

Zack,

I received your message and will respond in detail by this afternoon.

Rona

--
Rona Jackson
Assistant Vice President
Accounting Department
Tel: (212) 555-7654
Fax: (212) 555-3456

Figure 8 • A BRIEF BUT COURTEOUS E-MAIL MESSAGE

Chapter 4
Organization Matters

Time-tested principles of good business writing, including those governing organization, apply to e-mail as well. Just like a memo, or report, or speech, a longer e-mail should generally have an introduction, a body, and a conclusion.

For shorter e-mails, many of the same organizational principles apply, but in a highly compressed form. This chapter considers structural issues in both long and short e-mail messages.

4.1 Get to the Point Quickly

No matter how long or short the e-mail, your readers should always be able to understand right away why you are writing to them. Are you responding to a previous message from the recipient? Do you need a particular file? Are you trying to set up a meeting? Do you want to convince your manager that you need a BlackBerry?

Whether your e-mail message is two sentences or six paragraphs in length, you should clearly state the main point of your message — and state it right away. It is possible to send a perfectly sound e-mail just one sentence in length, as long as that sentence clearly expresses your purpose. If your e-mail consists of several paragraphs, your main point should appear within the first paragraph of the e-mail.

If at first you can't figure out how to express your main idea economically, you should keep writing and rewriting until you can. You may find it necessary to revise your main idea multiple times before it conveys the point of your e-mail message in a concise, clear, interesting way.

Sometimes people get to the point too quickly, as illustrated in Figure 9.

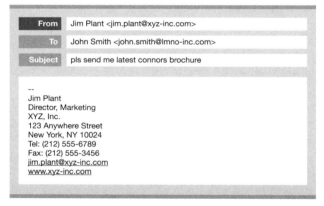

Figure 9 • ABRUPT E-MAIL MESSAGE

The only content appears in the subject line, therefore violating the average reader's expectation of finding the main point in the main e-mail window. It is possible the recipient may even think that the message was sent in error and delete it. Finally, the abruptness of the message — the absence of any salutation or closing — may offend the reader.

Compare the original e-mail in Figure 9 with the much improved version in Figure 10.

From	Jim Plant <jim.plant@xyz-inc.com>
To	John Smith <john.smith@lmno-inc.com>
Subject	Connors brochure

John,

I would like to have a copy of the Connors brochure for my 5:00 meeting with Samantha. Would you please e-mail me the latest draft as soon as you receive this message?

Thank you,
Jim

--
Jim Plant
Director, Marketing
XYZ, Inc.
123 Anywhere Street
New York, NY 10024
Tel: (212) 555-6789
Fax: (212) 555-3456
jim.plant@xyz-inc.com
www.xyz-inc.com

Figure 10 • FORMERLY ABRUPT E-MAIL: REVISED VERSION

The average recipient would be more likely to read and respond to such a message. In addition, there is no longer a danger that the recipient will be offended by the message. The writer addresses the reader by name, clarifies the point so that it is immediately accessible, and concludes by thanking him.

4.2 Paragraph Length

Have you ever received an e-mail message that consists of a single extremely long paragraph? If so, perhaps you will be able to sympathize with the many readers who find long, bulky paragraphs exhausting, especially on the computer screen.

A body paragraph — in other words, any paragraph falling between the introduction and conclusion — should generally contain one main idea on which the writer elaborates. There are exceptions, but many paragraphs follow this format, and many of those that don't, should.

When you signal the start of a new paragraph (in e-mail, by skipping a line), you are signaling to the reader the start of a new thought. Paragraphing is an example of how form — in other words, an e-mail's appearance — supports content. A very long paragraph suggests the writer has included too many ideas in a single block, thus leaving it up to the recipient to understand which sentences go together and how the various ideas relate to one another.

On average, e-mail messages are shorter and more frequent than business correspondence of the past. It is not unusual to find a series of quite short paragraphs in good e-mail messages (though it is common for people to think, mistakenly, that e-mail paragraphs are shorter than they are, simply because of the way many e-mail software programs display the text across the width of the computer screen).

Although an accumulation of excessively short paragraphs can sometimes be problematic, creating a choppy effect, many effective e-mail messages consist of several short paragraphs, each in turn consisting of no more than a sentence or two.

4.3 **Order of Ideas**

The order of ideas in the body of a document, electronic or otherwise (here *body* refers to everything between the introduction and conclusion), is based on content and goals. However, your ideas should unfold in a way that makes sense and is readily accessible to the reader.

Particularly for longer e-mail messages, it can be helpful to keep in mind these general organizational principles:

1. In many e-mails, the most important ideas should appear first, with less important ideas appearing later.

Why? Your reader will be more likely to continue reading if the ideas seem significant. In addition, if your reader is unavoidably interrupted, at least he or she will have read your most important points.

2. In other e-mails, ideas appear in a logical chain.

In an e-mail about a technical topic, for example, you may be explaining complex ideas to people who are unfamiliar with your subject matter. To succeed, you must think like a teacher, introducing ideas one at a time to your audience and explaining each one clearly before you move on to the next. You may actually end up developing your most important idea last—after you have explained all the preceding concepts the reader must understand in order to grasp your big idea.

A cautionary note: where you develop the big idea last, you should still have at least introduced this core theme in your e-mail's opening lines.

3. Content can also be presented in chronological order.

Many e-mail messages contain short narratives, details, or examples that are generally best explained in chronological order. In other words, the writer starts at the beginning, proceeds to the middle, and concludes with the end. An anecdote or example can last a couple of sentences or multiple paragraphs. Unfortunately, some businesspeople overuse chronological structures in cases where another organizational principle — principle 1 on the previous page, for example — might be better.

These principles apply even to the very compressed form of a shorter e-mail, where the writer won't necessarily have a separate introductory paragraph. Imagine, for example, that you are writing an e-mail to your manager, Mindy. You have researched some new technology, and you have concluded that investing $10,000 in new hardware and software will save your department about $30,000 per year in support costs. You have written and are attaching a two-page report describing the new technology and detailing the cost reductions.

There are a couple of ways someone might try to structure such an e-mail. The approach in Figure 11 on the next page is a very common one, but is not as effective as the approach in Figure 12.

In Figure 11, the writer, Marcia, presents the information chronologically. In other words, what happens first — the spending or the savings? The spending, of course, and it is the spending that leads

Figure 11 • CHRONOLOGICAL ORDER OF IDEAS

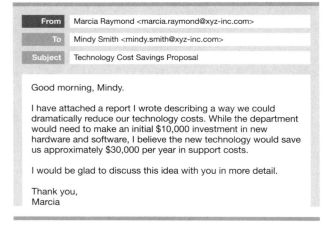

Figure 12 • MOST IMPORTANT IDEA FIRST

the e-mail. Though the writer quickly proceeds to the savings, what happens if the reader, Mindy, is very busy, or feels concerned about the tight budget, or is about to be interrupted by a phone call? She may focus too much on the spending first, without ever reaching the savings benefit.

The second e-mail, on the other hand, follows the first organizational principle described above; it puts the most important idea — the savings — first. The initial ideas actually appear in reverse chronological order, moving from what happens second (the savings) to what happens first (the spending). For the sake of getting the big idea across right away, it makes sense to reverse the chronology so that something engaging and important can launch the e-mail. The new emphasis is apparent in the shift in subject line as well; the weaker *New Technology Purchases* in Figure 11 is replaced with *Technology Cost Savings Proposal* in Figure 12.

The approach used in Figure 12 makes it more likely that Mindy will respond favorably, and efficiently, to the request for the purchases.

Keep in mind that, especially with long e-mail messages, the choice of organizational structure is not necessarily an all-or-nothing decision. Principle 1 may be at work in one section of an e-mail while 2 or 3 dominates in another section.

4.4 **Development**

Even in the relatively compressed form of an e-mail, you must explain your ideas adequately; in other words, you must *develop* them. The reader should not have to work to understand what you mean; rather, you — the writer — should do the work for the reader.

Thus, complex points must be allotted time and space sufficient for the reader to understand them. General statements should be supported with details and examples.

Consider the following paragraph from a hypothetical e-mail message:

> We must do a better job of meeting customer needs.
> For example, we have to respond more quickly and
> professionally to customer requests for assistance.

At first glance, the paragraph may seem to contain the supporting details necessary to explain its main idea, that we should do a better job of meeting customer needs. What, however, does *more quickly and professionally* mean?

Now compare the paragraph below with the preceding example.

> We must do a better job of meeting customer needs.
> When a customer calls or e-mails with a problem or
> complaint, we need to resolve the issue within 24

hours. In addition, we should follow up with a phone call within five days of an initial inquiry to ensure that the customer is satisfied with the resolution.

The revised version contains concrete, useful details. Although the first version did not develop its main idea, the second does.

4.5 **Bulleting**

Bullets can help organize information visually so that it is easier to read. In e-mail, bullet points are often a useful way to present material consisting of a series of items or otherwise list-like information. Compare the messages in Figures 13 and 14.

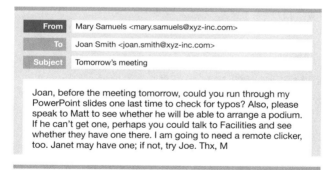

From	Mary Samuels <mary.samuels@xyz-inc.com>
To	Joan Smith <joan.smith@xyz-inc.com>
Subject	Tomorrow's meeting

Joan, before the meeting tomorrow, could you run through my PowerPoint slides one last time to check for typos? Also, please speak to Matt to see whether he will be able to arrange a podium. If he can't get one, perhaps you could talk to Facilities and see whether they have one there. I am going to need a remote clicker, too. Janet may have one; if not, try Joe. Thx, M

Figure 13 • LIST OF TASKS WITHOUT BULLETS

The e-mail in Figure 14 is much easier to read—and therefore more likely to get the kind of organized, systematic response Mary would presumably like from Joan.

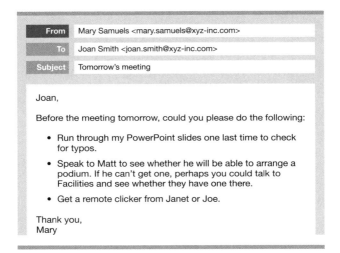

From	Mary Samuels <mary.samuels@xyz-inc.com>
To	Joan Smith <joan.smith@xyz-inc.com>
Subject	Tomorrow's meeting

Joan,

Before the meeting tomorrow, could you please do the following:

- Run through my PowerPoint slides one last time to check for typos.
- Speak to Matt to see whether he will be able to arrange a podium. If he can't get one, perhaps you could talk to Facilities and see whether they have one there.
- Get a remote clicker from Janet or Joe.

Thank you,
Mary

Figure 14 • REVISED LIST OF TASKS, WITH BULLETS

One problem with bullets is that some people use them to excess. The effect can be staccato and not particularly warm. Make sure you have enough text framing your bullet points so that your e-mail sounds like you and not just a series of lists.

A format warning: bulleting isn't always preserved on the recipient's end, so consider using plain old hyphens in lieu of bullets. They aren't pretty, but they won't get garbled during transmission.

4.6 **Long E-Mail Messages**

If you have multiple pages of information to e-mail (for example, a report, memo, proposal, or other business document), consider sending them in the form of an attachment. It is much easier to edit a large volume of text in, say, Microsoft Word, than in the body of a typical e-mail.

Your information will probably also look better in an attachment. Although it is usually possible to format text in the body of your e-mail, if recipients have a different type of e-mail software, the message may not look the same on their end as on yours. With an attachment, the formatting will remain more or less as you leave it. In fact, you can ensure that the format doesn't shift by sending the attachment as a PDF file (a file format created with Adobe Acrobat software).

By using attachments, you can send polished, professional-looking documents — without having to sacrifice the speed and ease of e-mail. See Section 7.6 for additional comments on sending e-mail attachments.

4.7 **Conclusions**

In a formal business document, the conclusion ties together your main ideas. Most e-mails, though, do not require a formal conclusion. Often a concluding paragraph consists of just a sentence or two in which, for example, the writer thanks the recipient or offers assistance. See Section 5.2.4 for guidance on word choice in closing sentences.

Chapter 5
Editing Your E-Mail

Consider the days of typewriters, when a businessperson would type a letter, then maybe retype it, address an envelope, lick a stamp, and find a mailbox. A typed, and maybe retyped, letter tended to elicit from its writer a greater commitment to editing than the average e-mail does today.

There is much to recommend e-mail efficiency, but for e-mail that matters, the best approach is to treat it with the same care you would give to a printed, mailed letter or companywide memo. Plan your structure carefully, revise after you write, proofread, print, reread, and, if necessary, revise, print, and reread again. The more careful habits of the typewriter age can ensure greater professionalism and effectiveness in the e-mail age, too.

Before you click "Send," check your e-mail not only for organization, as discussed in the preceding chapter, but also for sentence structure, word choice, and grammar. Problems in these areas are responsible for much of the lack of clarity in business e-mail today.

Some e-mailers are concerned that they are too slow. They look around and see people flinging out five e-mail messages in the time that it takes them to write one. Unless you aren't getting your work done, don't concern yourself with this discrepancy. Many of the people who are shipping out e-mail messages as fast as they can type should slow down, and some of the very best e-mailers are those who compose and edit with care. Remember the story of the tortoise and the hare.

5.1 **Sentence Structure**

Good sentence structure is essential to good writing; it adds both clarity and interest. Poor sentence structure can befuddle or weary the audience, making the task of reading more unpleasant than informative.

5.1.1 *Sentence Variety*

One important way to enliven a piece of writing is to vary the length and structure of your sentences. Try reading aloud something you have written. Listen to the rhythm and flow of the sentences. Is there interest and variety? Or do you feel as though there is a kind of repetitive drone? If the latter is the case, you may be in a sentence structure rut! Try mixing things up a bit. Vary sentence length. Vary the way you combine ideas.

Many e-mailers looking for efficiency try to cram as much information as possible into a single long sentence. That approach is a misguided one. In overusing long, convoluted sentences, writers obscure their ideas behind complex syntax. Busy professionals simply do not want to reread sentences to try to figure out what the writer meant.

On the other hand, if a piece of writing contains too many short, simple sentences in a row, the writing may sound choppy and unsophisticated.

Variety adds interest. A simple, punchy idea may be best expressed with a simple sentence structure. A more complicated idea may justify a longer, more complex sentence structure. A mixture of sentence types can make the act of reading your e-mail a more pleasurable and productive experience for your audience.

Consider the following ideas, for example:

Employees have been complaining about the
lack of local restaurants. We have decided to build
a cafeteria on Lot 5.

These two ideas can be combined into a single sentence in a number of ways, each of which has a different rhythm, emphasis, and style. Read the following sentences aloud so that you can hear the differences among them.

Version 1. Employees have been complaining about the lack of local restaurants, so we have decided to build a cafeteria on Lot 5.

Version 2. Employees have been complaining about the lack of local restaurants; therefore, we have decided to build a cafeteria on Lot 5.

Version 3. We have decided to build a cafeteria on Lot 5 because employees have been complaining about the lack of local restaurants.

Version 4. Because employees have been complaining about the lack of local restaurants, we have decided to build a cafeteria on Lot 5.

Don't be concerned about beginning a sentence with *because,* as in Version 4. Unfortunately, many people are told as children not to use this word to start a sentence. Though the advice often comes from well-intentioned teachers, it is wrong—and often very limiting for adult writers. Professional writers use this structure regularly, and with impunity. Needless avoidance of this perfectly good structure reduces the rhythmic variety of your writing and also, depending on what techniques a person uses to avoid it, can lead to unwieldy and inferior sentences such as the following:

Weak

Due to the fact that employees have been complaining about the lack of local restaurants, we have decided to build a cafeteria on Lot 5.

The preceding sentence is inherently inferior to Version 4; it is wordier and unnecessarily convoluted. Clean, direct sentences are critical for crisp, clear writing.

5.1.2 *The Dreaded Comma Splice*

Many e-mailers today are in the habit of combining two independent clauses — complete thoughts that could stand alone as their own sentences — with just a comma, like this:

> Revenues were plummeting, we decided to
> close two branches.

Unfortunately, the sentence above is actually a sentence error called a *comma splice*. If you are writing a creative piece — a poem or novel, for example — you may occasionally find stylistic reasons to use a comma splice. Business writing, however, is a place for traditional punctuation, not experimentation.

Think of the comma as being too frail, too delicate a piece of punctuation, to hold apart two independent clauses without the additional help of some kind of combining word. In business writing, where you can put a period you can virtually never put a comma. If you do, you will usually create a comma splice. Periods and commas are like punctuation enemies; though they may be distant relatives, they do not get along and do not hang out in the same kinds of places.

5.1.3 *Passive Voice*

Perhaps you have been told before not to use passive voice, examples of which abound in business writing. The idea, though, is not to eliminate passive voice entirely; rather, you should avoid excessive or unjustified use of passive voice.

> ■ DEFINING PASSIVE VOICE

To reduce passive voice, one must first be able to identify it. The sentence below offers a classic example:

> The proposals were evaluated by the marketing committee.

This sentence is an example of passive voice because it possesses the following characteristics:

1. The grammatical subject—*proposals*, in this example—receives the action of the verb. In other words, the proposals don't do anything; something is done to them.

2. The verbs include the following:

   a. a form of the verb *to be* (*were*, in this case). Besides *were*, other forms of *to be* are as follows: *am, is, are, was, be, been*, and *being*.

   b. a **past participle** (here, the word *evaluated*)

In case the past participle is a hazy memory—as it is for many people—just remember that it is the form of a verb that would fit in the following blank: *I have* _____. For regular verbs, the past participle is identical to the past tense (*I have walked* vs. *I walked*, *I have finished* vs. *I finished*, etc.). For irregular verbs, the past participle and past tense differ. For instance, the past participle of *to run* is *run*, while the past tense is *ran*. The past participle of *to eat* is *eaten*, while the past tense is *ate*.

With passive voice, if the entity performing the action is included in the sentence, it typically follows the verbs and appears as part of a prepositional phrase (in the example above, *by the marketing committee*). A sentence can contain passive voice without including this information, though. Deleting *by the marketing committee* from the sample sentence does not eliminate the passive voice. The following is still a passive construction:

The proposals were evaluated.

As you look for passive voice, keep in mind that a form of the verb *to be* does not automatically signal a passive construction. For example, how many of the following three sentences contain passive voice?

1. The presentation was not applicable to my work.
2. The presentation was lost by the marketing department.

3. The presentation was boring the audience.

In fact, only the second sentence illustrates passive voice. In Sentence 1, *applicable* is an adjective, not a past participle. In the third sentence, *boring* is not a past participle either (it can't fit in the following blank: *I have* _____). In addition, the subject of the sentence—*presentation*—is performing the action, namely, boring the audience. Sentence 3 is actually an example of **active voice**.

■ REDUCING PASSIVE VOICE

In many passive-voice constructions, the writer would be better off rewriting the sentence using active voice. Compare these two versions:

Passive Voice

The proposals were evaluated by the marketing committee.

Active Voice

The marketing committee evaluated the proposals.

Active voice is generally superior to passive voice. For one thing, it is more direct. The reader learns first who or what performed the action, then what the action was, and finally who or what was acted upon. Generally it is easier to process information that way than it is to begin with the recipient of the action, then learn what the action was, and then find out who did it.

Also, replacing passive with active voice in the example above reduced the number of words by two. Active voice is usually the more economical structure.

Watch out for passive-voice constructions such as the following, which recur frequently in business documents:

- it is recommended that
- it has been decided that
- it has been observed that
- it was noted that

In many cases, these phrases are fillers and can simply be eliminated, often with little or no rewriting of the remainder of the sentences that contain them. Compare the original and revised versions of the following sentences (passive voice is italicized):

Original

It was decided that we need to cut costs by 30%.

Improved

We need to cut costs by 30%.

—*or*—

Unfortunately, we need to cut costs by 30%.

Original

It has been observed that the employee break room is unacceptably messy by the end of the day.

Improved

The employee break room is unacceptably messy by the end of the day.

■ Acceptable Passive Voice

Nonetheless, passive voice is sometimes acceptable, even preferable. For example, it is appropriate in the following cases:

■ when the entity performing the action is unknown

Suppose your dog comes home one night with a cut on his leg, and you don't know the cause of the injury. When you go into work the next day, you might tell your co-worker, "My dog was injured last night." If you don't know how your dog was injured, it is difficult to construct an active-voice version of this sentence. You might have to say something strange like, "A car, another dog, or something else altogether injured my dog last night."

■ when the emphasis is properly on the entity receiving the action

For example, you might complain to a colleague in the marketing department, "Our website hasn't been updated in nearly a year." Here, passive voice emphasizes the fact that your website isn't current. Now, if you wanted to assign blame for this problem, you would probably gravitate towards active voice instead: "John and Mary haven't updated our website in nearly a year."

5.2 **Word Choice**

As you edit your e-mail, consider your word choice carefully, examining whether in any given case there is another word that could express an idea more clearly. Avoid the word choice problems described below.

5.2.1 *Vague Language*

Much business writing, e-mail included, suffers from a lack of precision. Why? In part because it is more difficult to be specific than it is to be vague. Specific writing requires more careful thought and more thoughtful writing and rewriting.

Compare the following two sentences:

Jon does consistently sloppy work.

Jon's reports consistently contain statistical and other factual errors.

In the first example, you have no way of knowing what exactly is meant by *sloppy*. Does Jon have messy handwriting? Does he spill his lunch on his reports? Or — a horrifying possibility — does he fail to proofread carefully?

The second example, by contrast, clearly identifies the problems with Jon's reports.

Editing for word choice problems requires a critical eye and attention to detail. It also requires a good dictionary. Most first drafts of e-mail messages will contain wording problems; the challenge is to revise so that the version you actually send says exactly what you want it to say.

5.2.2 *Wordiness and Ornate Language*

Writers sometimes use a hundred words where fifty would do. This tendency, known as wordiness, weakens writing in several ways.

First, it shows a lack of respect for the reader's time and suggests that the writer has not bothered to revise sufficiently. In business, wasted time means wasted money.

Second, verbosity obscures the writer's ideas by hiding them amid a word surplus. Is it easier to find a needle in a haystack or to find a needle amid a few wisps of straw?

Finally, wordiness frequently signals to the reader that the writer is seeking to hide a lack of substance.

Related to wordiness is the tendency to use unnaturally ornate expressions in an effort to dress up a piece of writing. Why write *is cognizant of* when you can substitute *is aware of* or *knows about*?

Why write *due to the fact that* when *because* will do? Straightforward, succinct language will draw less attention to itself and keep the reader's attention on your message.

E-mail correspondence frequently contains unnecessarily ornate expressions such as *please find attached* or *pursuant to your request*. Just as these expressions would sound stilted in speech, they sound stilted in written communications. Replace them with more direct, natural language, as illustrated in the table below.

Ornate Expression	More Natural Alternative
please find attached attached please find	I have attached *or* attached is
please be advised that	[nothing] *or* please note that
per your request as per your request pursuant to your request	as you requested
per our conversation as per our conversation	as we discussed

Eliminating problematic phrases can dramatically improve your writing style. Consider the effect of a few simple word-choice substitutions in the following pairs of sentences.

Unnecessarily Ornate	Revised
Pursuant to your request, please find attached the status report.	As you requested, I have attached the status report.
Please be advised that the meeting will begin at 4:00 instead of 3:30.	The meeting will begin at 4:00 instead of 3:30.
As per our conversation, I have asked Barbara to research the new location.	As we discussed, I have asked Barbara to research the new location.

5.2.3 Too Few Words

In trying to combat wordiness, many e-mailers head the opposite direction, using so few words that the reader can't understand what they are trying to say. Being concise doesn't mean using few words; it means using as few words as are needed. If you end up having a five-message exchange, spread out over two days, because your original e-mail was too terse, you haven't saved anyone any time.

The moral: don't be brief to the point of incomprehensibility. Your reader needs enough information to understand what you need or want.

Another often problematic habit in e-mail is to leave out words that are necessary grammatically, such as **articles** (*a, an,* and *the*) and **direct objects**.

For example, certain verbs require a direct object to complete their meaning, but direct objects are frequently omitted by e-mailers seeking to save keystrokes. Consider these sentences:

The attorney questioned her client.

The manager disappeared.

In the first sentence, *client* receives the action of the verb *questioned*. *Client* is thus the direct object; without it, the sentence is incomplete. In the second sentence, there is no noun or pronoun to receive the action of the verb *disappeared*; a direct object is unnecessary.

Depending on your company's culture, it may be acceptable to omit articles or direct objects for the sake of time or space in short, quick e-mail messages to longtime colleagues, particularly when you are all working on BlackBerrys or similar devices. For example:

Missing Direct Object

Please review.

Missing Article

Please review report.

The problem is, many people don't shift out of this mode when they are writing important e-mails that require more care and attention. In such e-mail messages, you should write the complete sentence, with no missing parts:

Complete Thought

Please review the report.

5.2.4 *Trite Language*

Trite language is language that has become stale through overuse. For example, clichés — trite expressions or sayings — are victims of their own popularity. If, at a meeting, you caution your colleague, "Don't throw the baby out with the bathwater," you are using a cliché to express your point. Trite language acts as a kind of verbal sedative. If the wording is that familiar to your reader, he or she will be able to complete your sentence without even bothering to read what you have written. That in turn suggests that what you have written is not necessarily all that original or important.

Trite language can also involve repeated words or phrases. There is a particular category of trite language common in e-mail and typically appearing at the end of messages in the form of stock phrases or sentences. For example:

Please feel free to call or e-mail me with any comments, questions, or suggestions.

The sentence is a bit wordy, though in isolation it is not terrible. The problem is that some people will use the identical sentence in virtually every e-mail, sometimes even embedding the sentence into a signature file to save time. If the e-mailer puts the same sentence in every e-mail, what is the effect? The etiquette benefits erode, and the sentence strikes the reader as insincere.

The idea behind such a sentence is a good one, but you might want to consider varying it, paring down the number of words, and excluding it from e-mails where it simply isn't relevant. Here are variations that could work in different e-mails:

I would be glad to answer any questions.

Please feel free to call or e-mail me with any comments or questions.

Please call or e-mail me with any questions.

Please call me with any suggestions.

You are welcome to call with questions or suggestions.

Writing can't always be automated, and when you do automate, you risk sounding inauthentic. Even subtle variations can make a big difference in your overall e-mail style.

5.3 **Editing Techniques**

Too many e-mailers do not review their e-mail messages before sending them. Others give their messages only the most cursory once-over before pressing "Send." Get in the habit of editing e-mail. Especially for important communications, it is critical to review your e-mail carefully before transmitting it to others. Some useful editing strategies appear below.

5.3.1 *Printing and Proofreading*

For most people, it is much easier to catch mistakes in a hard-copy document than it is to see them on a computer screen. If you are sending an important e-mail, print and review the message before sending it.

While some e-mail writers may find the extra step annoying and time-consuming, remember that your communication will likely be immortalized on company servers.

5.3.2 *Reading Aloud*

Before you send an e-mail, read it out loud to yourself. Reading aloud is an excellent technique to help you edit any type of writing, whether on a computer screen or on paper. It can help you notice missing words, problems with sentence structure, unnecessary repetition, and any number of other stylistic or grammatical issues.

5.3.3 *Spell-Checkers*

Most people, even excellent spellers, are far better off using their e-mail spell-checkers than not. True, spell-checkers can slow down the e-mail writing process — but more important, spelling errors can slow down the recipient's reading process! The benefits of using this technological tool outweigh the drawbacks of the delay. You may be surprised at how many typos or misspellings a spell-checker picks up.

A cautionary note, though: do not rush through the spell-checking process, automatically accepting every spelling suggestion offered to you. Spell-checkers have limitations and may suggest the wrong word for the context. In addition, there are numerous errors they may not notice at all. Suppose Jane means to type, *The ban was inadequate*, but it is late at night and she is tired, so instead she types:

The van was inadequate.

Your spell-checker will of course view this sentence as correct. A spell-checker isn't a substitute for careful proofreading.

EDITING TIP
....

Many people have experienced the horror of mistakenly hitting the "Send" key and dispatching an e-mail before it was ready. To prevent this problem, leave the *To* field blank or fill it in with your own address until you have completed the editing process.

5.3.4 *Editing Partners*

For important e-mails, consider setting up an editing partnership with a colleague. You can read each other's high-priority e-mail messages and, working as a team, improve overall correspondence quality.

For very significant e-mail communications, it may be a good idea for your department to set up an official system with assigned editing partners and standard review procedures. Such a system can help prevent major errors.

5.3.5 *Breaks*

Good writers know the importance of breaks to writing quality. Have you ever struggled with a document and decided to put it away for a while, only to discover when you return to it that you have found a solution to whatever writing problem was plaguing you?

If you have to write three e-mails before lunch, consider writing drafts of all three of them, then cycling back through them one at a time and editing each message before you send it. Having even five minutes away from an e-mail can help you spot mistakes that you didn't notice when you composed it.

On the other hand, if you write one in its entirety, read it, then send it, then start the second, completing and sending it before you begin the third, you won't have a chance to look at any of them with fresh eyes.

The drafting approach proposed here doesn't need to add time to the e-mail process; in fact, some people find it more efficient because they edit more rapidly when they have a little distance from what they have written.

Chapter 6

Relationship
Management

E-MAIL ENABLES PROFESSIONALS TO COMMUNICATE EFFICIENTLY with a broad network of people, independent of time zones and geographical constraints. Nonetheless, electronic communications should not be viewed as an all-purpose replacement for conversation. Live interactions, whether on the phone or in person, are valuable tools for building and sustaining professional relationships that can help you throughout your career.

Therefore, don't overestimate the utility of e-mail. And, when you do use it, use it wisely. Below are some guidelines on managing relationships effectively through e-mail.

1. Don't barricade yourself behind your computer.

In this electronic age, people sometimes fail to recognize the value of spoken communications, whether on the phone or in person. Preferring e-mail, they avoid face-to-face or phone conversations. This strategy is unwise. For one thing, it may cause you to be perceived as aloof or inaccessible. In addition, having a conversation is in some cases more efficient than e-mailing, particularly for issues requiring significant discussion. E-mail should complement rather than replace the spoken word.

2. Be responsive to your clients' and managers' communication preferences.

Regardless of your own preferences, be sensitive to the communication preferences of your clients and managers. If some of them prefer to communicate through e-mail rather than by phone, for example, communicate with them by e-mail as much as is possible or reasonable. You may think — or know — that e-mailing will be less efficient than talking by phone, but proceed with caution in overriding their preferences.

This applies to stylistic choices within e-mail, too. For example, although it is generally unwise to bundle multiple unrelated issues into a single message, if your manager tells you that he or she prefers a single long summary e-mail each day, you should respect that preference.

3. Don't rely solely on e-mail to communicate about critical subjects.

To communicate with someone about a really important issue — an imminent major deadline, for example — don't assume an e-mail will be enough.

In such cases, try phoning instead of or in addition to e-mailing. You can't assume people will see and respond to e-mail quickly, especially not if they travel a lot or receive dozens of e-mail messages a day. If you are e-mailing someone you don't know well with an urgent request for information, make sure your phone number appears in the message; including it will increase the likelihood that you get an efficient response.

4. Remember that your e-mail communications represent you in your absence.

If you are writing to your clients or managers, pay even more attention than you normally would to e-mail quality.

That doesn't mean that the other e-mails — to your employees, vendors, and so on — don't matter. How you treat other people reflects on you. People who habitually send careless messages — messages that are confusing, or unclear, or in which the name of the recipient is misspelled — to people over whom they have power may be sending a message that those relationships don't matter much to them. Good e-mail skills are part of good management skills.

5. Don't boss the boss.

In writing to your boss, avoid using the imperative mode — in other words, the command form of a verb. Within the bounds of reason and law, the boss can, after all, do what the boss wants. The following are all examples of commands.

> Let me know what you think.
>
> Please let me know what you think.
>
> Review the attached document.
>
> Please review the attached document.

While the *Please* in the second and fourth sentences adds courtesy, the inclusion of that word doesn't change the fact that these sentences are commands, and hence not generally ideal for communications to one's boss.

Try one of the following instead:

> I would be glad to answer any questions.
>
> I would welcome your comments.
>
> I will check in with you later this week to see whether you'd like to discuss the document in more detail.
>
> Please let me know if you have any questions.

Grammatically the last sentence is actually a command, too, but this type of sentence amounts essentially to a veiled offer—you would be glad to answer questions—and therefore sounds courteous rather than bossy.

Your current manager may be oblivious to such

linguistic nuances. Nonetheless, it's good defensive e-mailing to observe this guideline, as you may well encounter a manager in the future who is not oblivious.

6. Don't use e-mail to communicate about sensitive or inflammatory topics.

Be sensible about the types of subjects you try to address through e-mail. If you sense that an e-mail dialogue is becoming confrontational, stop communicating about the topic online and have a phone conversation — or, even better — a face-to-face discussion with the person. It is usually less effective to communicate about sensitive topics through the medium of the computer than it is to speak in person or over the phone. By talking things through, you are more likely to keep a situation from spiraling out of control.

Chapter 7
Special Topics

E-mail offers powerful communication capabilities — but also some attendant risks and challenges. This chapter addresses some of the communication issues unique to e-mail.

7.1 **Automatic Replies**

An automatic reply is the message a person sets up
to go out automatically in response to any e-mails
that arrive, often though not necessarily while he
or she is out of the office. Auto-replies pose two
key challenges:

1. Many people compose them in a rush right
before they go away on a business trip or vacation.
It is very difficult to write a good e-mail while rush-
ing.

2. With most e-mails, you know the audience.
With auto-replies, you are trying to anticipate all the
people who might be e-mailing you and compose
something suitable for a wide range of readers.

In 2003, job applicants who submitted an

electronic message to an e-mail address on the website of a major U.S. financial firm received an automatic reply whose subject line assured them that their submission had been *recieved* (rather than *received*—the correct spelling). Unfortunately, basic misspellings, typos, and other mistakes are common in auto-replies.

In composing your auto-reply, ask yourself who might write to you. What do they need to know? What should they not know?

Below are some guidelines to keep in mind when you set up an auto-reply:

- Compose it well ahead of time so that you are not too rushed to review it carefully.

- Make sure your automatic response is turned off as soon as you return from your trip, or wherever you happen to have been. It is undesirable to have messages going out on December 20 announcing that you will return on December 17.

- Provide neither too much information nor too little. It is fine for someone to explain that she is out for a month on maternity leave. In other cases, people may choose to exclude the reason they are away from the office. As a general rule, keep the information minimal. After all, you don't know who will be writing to you—and thus reading whatever message goes out automatically.

■ If relevant or necessary, you may want to explain how people can reach you in case of emergency. If you are still going to be checking your e-mail every evening, consider saying so (unless you won't have time to reply!). If you are not going to check your e-mail at all but you will check your voicemail regularly, you might say that.

■ Generally you should not include a complete signature file in an auto-reply, especially if you are in a role where you regularly receive unsolicited messages from salespeople and other strangers. However, you should conclude the e-mail with a kind of basic signature file that includes at least your full name and your company. You may also want to add your title or department. The idea is to include enough information to help colleagues and clients who try to reach you, but not so much that people you don't know — and don't want to know — will be able to collect information such as your phone number, fax, and so on.

■ Check your message for clarity and accuracy.

■ Check for spelling, grammar, and format.

■ Check for tone; the auto-reply should be polite.

■ Do not include contact information for others at your firm unless you are certain it is acceptable to do so. If you are providing contact information for people who work *for* you, you can presumably offer this information without asking permission, though you should tell them that you are doing so. Before sending out contact information for colleagues or bosses, however, make sure you have their permission to include this information in your auto-reply. You don't want to flood unsuspecting co-workers with unwanted messages; you also want them to be prepared so that they can respond professionally to calls or messages normally intended for you.

Figure 15 offers an example of an effective auto-reply. The subject line is specific, meaning that the recipient, Karen Jones, won't even have to read the message to know that the person she just e-mailed, Jack, is away from his office. When Karen does read it, she will know when Jack will be back and whom to call if she needs help before then. The message is clear, simple, and specific.

In addition, the signature file is abbreviated, omitting phone, fax, and other contact details. There is no salutation, simply because it is difficult to compose a greeting appropriate for the entire spectrum of potential correspondents. (An auto-reply is one of the few cases where the absence of such a greeting is broadly acceptable, but if you like, you may add a line at the beginning that reads *Greetings*.)

Finally, the tone of this auto-reply is professional

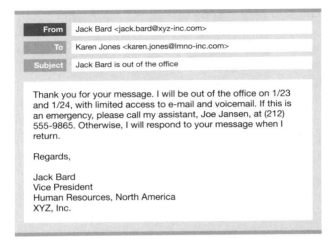

From	Jack Bard <jack.bard@xyz-inc.com>
To	Karen Jones <karen.jones@lmno-inc.com>
Subject	Jack Bard is out of the office

Thank you for your message. I will be out of the office on 1/23 and 1/24, with limited access to e-mail and voicemail. If this is an emergency, please call my assistant, Joe Jansen, at (212) 555-9865. Otherwise, I will respond to your message when I return.

Regards,

Jack Bard
Vice President
Human Resources, North America
XYZ, Inc.

Figure 15 • AUTO-REPLY

and polite. In it, Jack Bard thanks any person who e-mails him during his absence. Now, under normal circumstances, you may not feel like thanking everyone who sends you an e-mail message (especially if it's a chain letter or an invitation to participate in what sounds suspiciously like a pyramid scheme), but that's fine. You can simply delete those annoying messages when you return.

If you subscribe to a listserv—a mailing list program for communicating with other people who have subscribed to the same list—remember to unsubscribe before you set up an auto-reply. Otherwise, every time you receive an e-mail from the list, other subscribers will receive an auto-reply from you telling them you are away. Imprecations have rained down on the heads of hapless vacationers who forgot to unsubscribe from listservs before departing for a week of skiing or sunbathing.

7.2 **Copying**

Use the *Cc* field to copy people who need the information in a given message, but who don't need to respond themselves. If you are writing to two people who both need to respond to your message, don't use the *Cc* field; instead, put both e-mail addresses in the *To* field.

If you are sending an e-mail to two people, one of whom appears in the *To* field and the other of whom appears in the *Cc* field, address only the person in the *To* field in your salutation. If the recipient in the *To* field doesn't know the copied person, it is generally a good idea to explain who the person is and why you are copying him or her, as shown in Figure 16.

Don't overuse the copying feature of e-mail. See Chapter 8, "Reducing E-Mail Volume," for a discussion of copying as a contributor to excessive e-mail volume.

7.3 **Blind Copying**

Blind copying enables you to copy someone on a message without allowing the main recipient to see

From	Sue Jones <sue.jones@xyz-inc.com>
To	Jane Smith <jane.smith@lmno-inc.com>
Cc	Tom Roberts <tom.roberts@xyz-inc.com>
Subject	re: Subscription problems

Dear Ms. Smith:

I am sorry to hear that you have been having trouble with your subscription. I am researching the problem and have copied my manager, Tom Roberts, so that he is aware of the situation.

I will follow up with you by Monday at the latest.

Sincerely,

Sue Jones
Customer Service
XYZ, Inc.
Tel: (800) 555-2100, ext. 380
Fax: (348) 555-2109
sue.jones@xyz-inc.com
www.xyz-inc.com

Figure 16 • E-Mail Copying a Manager

that someone else has received the message. It is the *Bcc* field (standing for *blind carbon copy*) on an e-mail.

The *Bcc* field can be very useful for certain types of group mailings. When you send out messages to multiple people who do not know each other—for instance, a group of your company's vendors—you can use the *Bcc* field to ensure that their e-mail addresses are not revealed. If you don't, in the worst-case scenario unscrupulous individuals may take those addresses and put them on their own mailing lists. Even if that doesn't happen, though, it is simply good business to respect the privacy of the people you e-mail.

Otherwise, be cautious in using the blind copying feature, as it is sometimes employed in ways that test the limits of business etiquette and ethics. Generally you should not blind copy someone if the recipient in the *To* field would be disturbed to discover that that person was surreptitiously included in the communication. If the blind copying does not serve an ethical and legitimate business purpose, avoid it. This issue becomes even more pressing if the recipient's own messages are being passed on, without his or her knowledge, as part of an ongoing e-mail dialogue that is being shared with invisible participants.

Finally, there is a technical issue to consider: if a blind-copied person clicks "Reply All" and sends a response, the original recipient may well receive that message, which would in turn reveal that the original sender blind copied someone on the e-mail—a potential source of offense. A safer alternative is to send the original e-mail, then go to your Sent box and forward the message to the third person.

7.4 **Forwarding**

The ability to forward e-mail messages is a powerful feature that allows information to be shared quickly with others. But the fact that e-mail can be forwarded so easily creates business communication challenges that did not exist in the past.

One of the most disturbing habits in modern business correspondence is the unexamined forwarding of messages that were intended for the original recipient and not for a broader audience. Before you press "Forward," consider carefully how the sender of the message would feel about having that e-mail passed on to another reader.

At the same time, a healthy sense of self-preservation should inspire you to avoid *writing* e-mails that you yourself wouldn't want to have forwarded. E-mail does get forwarded, so it is simply good defensive e-mailing to avoid saying anything inappropriate, contentious, or undiplomatic in a work-related message.

7.4.1 *When Not to Forward*

Whether it is acceptable to forward a given message depends on myriad factors, including the relationship between the writer and recipient, their relative status, and the content and context of the message. But in all cases it is important to remember that forwarding something private or sensitive is often likely to reflect poorly not only on the writer, but also on the person who forwards the message.

Proceed with caution when you are contemplating forwarding an e-mail from anyone, but be particularly cautious when the e-mail is from someone senior to you. In general, don't forward messages containing:

■ **Personal content.** Professionals should not embed personal information in business e-mails, but when they do, think twice (or thrice) before passing it on.

■ **Confidential information.** Be very careful in your treatment of sensitive personnel information. The same caveat applies to confidential business information that is meant only for your eyes or for the eyes of a select few people at your firm.

■ **Lengthy dialogues.** It is inefficient to forward a long dialogue when all the recipient needs is a subset of the information from the ongoing exchange. Instead of forwarding, consider writing a synthesis of the key issues. If you do forward an e-mail that contains a series of e-mail exchanges, make sure the entire dialogue is appropriate for forwarding. There may be sensitive content further down the page; check before sharing it with others.

■ **Content that is worded in a way that might not suit a different audience.** Be aware of the writer's intended audience. Someone writing quickly to a colleague might word things with less care than he or she would have taken in writing to a manager. Passing on an e-mail that the sender might have preferred to edit a bit more before sharing with others may be viewed as a violation of e-mail etiquette.

7.4.2 *Making Your Messages Forwardable*

Any e-mail you send can be forwarded. That fact has caused people to lose their jobs, so it is wise to be cautious about what you put in writing. Don't e-mail inflammatory content. In addition, structure your e-mails so that they can easily be forwarded for maximum benefit.

How does one do that? For one thing, it helps to divide multiple topics into multiple e-mails. In Figure 17 on the following page, the writer of the e-mail fails to take this advice and combines a message about a report he has been working on with an apology for arriving late to a morning meeting.

The first part of the e-mail discusses a revision of an online marketing report, a subject likely to be of interest to other employees of the company. It is quite possible, therefore, that the message will be forwarded. If the writer did a good job on the revision mentioned in the e-mail, the forwarding may well benefit him professionally.

Unfortunately, though, if this e-mail is forwarded in its current form, the allusion to his tardiness will automatically be passed on as well. Instead of

From | George Chen <george.chen@xyz-inc.com>
To | Karen James <karen.james@xyx-inc.com>
Subject | Revision of Online Marketing Report

Karen,

I have attached the latest revision of the online marketing report for your review. I made some substantial changes, including the following:

- deleted several paragraphs in Section 4 that repeated content in Section 2
- added an executive summary
- added various subheadings to help clarify organization

I look forward to hearing your response.

By the way, I'm very sorry I didn't arrive on time for the meeting this morning. My daughter has bronchitis, and I had to take her to the pediatrician on my way to work.

Regards,
George

--
George Chen
Marketing Department
Red Bank Facility
Tel: 918-555-4598
Fax: 918-555-8763

Figure 17 • Message That Can't Easily Be Forwarded

providing a purely positive reflection of his efforts on behalf of the company—exemplified by the report—the e-mail will inform people who would never have known it otherwise that he was tardy to a meeting that morning. The e-mail also contains personal information about family that the writer may not wish to share with others at his firm.

The writer would be better off doing one of two things: (1) splitting the e-mail into two messages, one addressing the report and another apologizing for the tardiness, or (2) sending an e-mail about the report and apologizing in person or over the phone for the tardiness. In either case, the content relating to the report could then be forwarded to people who may be impressed by it. They will not hear about tardiness, bronchitis, or other personal matters.

In a second example, shown in Figure 18 on the next page, the recipient is the sender's client. This e-mail is polite and clear, but it is less than ideal from a practical point of view. By covering two separate and unrelated issues — an upcoming project and an unpaid invoice — each of which requires the client to undertake a separate action, the writer reduces the chance that both actions will occur.

In fact, it is reasonably likely that the recipient will take care of one thing and then forget about the other. Because of the reference to the unpaid invoice, the recipient may forward the e-mail to the accounting department without remembering to answer the sender's question about the upcoming project. If the writer doesn't follow up quickly, she may lose the business!

In addition, the person in accounting who processes the sender's invoices really doesn't need to

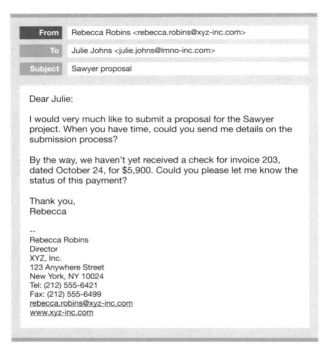

From	Rebecca Robins <rebecca.robins@xyz-inc.com>
To	Julie Johns <julie.johns@lmno-inc.com>
Subject	Sawyer proposal

Dear Julie:

I would very much like to submit a proposal for the Sawyer project. When you have time, could you send me details on the submission process?

By the way, we haven't yet received a check for invoice 203, dated October 24, for $5,900. Could you please let me know the status of this payment?

Thank you,
Rebecca

--
Rebecca Robins
Director
XYZ, Inc.
123 Anywhere Street
New York, NY 10024
Tel: (212) 555-6421
Fax: (212) 555-6499
rebecca.robins@xyz-inc.com
www.xyz-inc.com

Figure 18 • MESSAGE THAT BUNDLES TWO IDEAS INTO ONE

know that she is bidding on a new project. All the person in accounting needs is information on the late payment.

It is a sound business writing practice to include no more information in an e-mail than is relevant to your relationship with the original recipient and anyone else to whom your message is likely to be forwarded.

7.5 **Managing E-Mail Dialogues**

In most cases, it is helpful to set your e-mail software preferences so that your e-mail responses automatically include the message to which you are replying. Many people in a business environment receive scores of e-mail messages each day, and it can be difficult to keep track of ongoing dialogues with numerous people. By including previous messages in your reply, you remind recipients of the context and allow them to refer back easily to previous correspondence. Otherwise you may send them searching for earlier messages, or you may find that you waste valuable time in follow-up communications to clarify your point.

In managing an ongoing dialogue, it can sometimes be helpful to change subject lines periodically to reflect evolving subject matter. That may make it easier to find relevant e-mail messages later.

If the dialogue grows very long, you might consider deleting some messages from the bottom of the ongoing exchange — as long as you feel confident that the omission won't cause problems later if you need to look at the history of the discussion. In addition, you might want to leave out salutations and signature files after the dialogue is established, though in writing to clients or managers, you should probably follow their lead before dispensing with these elements.

7.6 **Attachments**

If you attach something to an e-mail, it is usually a good practice to include at least a line in the body of the e-mail telling the recipient what you've attached. For example, suppose an employee in a company's billing department e-mails an invoice to a client, but doesn't identify the attachment or include any text in the e-mail body. The recipient may think it is a virus and delete the e-mail without ever opening the attachment.

Or, suppose you e-mail a request for a file on a Wednesday, and the recipient doesn't reply with the attachment until Friday. Aside from the tardiness of the response—potentially problematic in itself—the person includes no explanatory comment of any type in the body of the message; he simply attaches the requested document. By this point, you may well no longer remember that you requested something from the recipient. The writer should therefore clarify the purpose of the e-mail and identify what is attached to it. Usually, though not in every case, information about the attachment should appear in the very first lines of the message. See Section 5.2.2 for recommendations on how to word such sentences.

Before you send an attachment, double-check that you have attached the right file. Open it just to be sure.

7.7 **Handheld Devices**

Workers on the move enjoy the convenience of handheld devices such as Treos and BlackBerrys that enable them to send and receive e-mail from wherever they are. Unfortunately, it is not easy to compose articulate messages on these tiny devices. That fact is no excuse, however, for a lack of clarity or an unprofessional format. You should in most cases still adhere to the standard guidelines for appropriate e-mail messages, setting up proper signature files, proofing for grammar and punctuation, and so on.

In addition, test your handheld device, often called a PDA (personal digital assistant), by sending a couple of messages to yourself and then scrutinizing their appearance on a normal-size monitor. The default format may need to be adjusted so that the PDA-generated e-mails look as professional as the messages you send from your desktop computer.

If you are a regular user of a handheld device, you know how difficult it can be to compose careful e-mail messages with those tiny keyboards. For e-mail that doesn't require an urgent reply, consider waiting until you are sitting at a desk with a full keyboard and monitor in front of you. If your work permits—and maybe it doesn't—you might consider using the device primarily for reading messages and not for writing. Some people read e-mail on their

PDAs and then respond via phone, if appropriate.

Another strategy is to purchase a foldout keyboard, if one is available for your device. They are small and portable, and can make typing responses much easier.

If you are not yourself a PDA user, but you regularly write e-mail to people who read your messages on such devices, you may want to make some adjustments to your standard e-mail habits for their convenience. Eliminating greetings, not necessarily skipping a line after a greeting, offering an abbreviated signature file, perhaps in some cases deleting the signature file altogether—all of these techniques can reduce the amount of time recipients must spend squinting and scrolling.

7.8 **E-Mail Templates**

If you repeatedly send out e-mails containing similar or identical content, you may find it convenient to automate the process by creating some e-mail templates, modifying them as necessary to suit a particular context. The technical aspects of setting them up will vary from one software program to the next, so if you need assistance, consult a tech-savvy colleague or your company's IT department.

If you do use templates and you are in the habit of customizing them for individual recipients, proofread each outgoing message with care and in its entirety. Templates can save time, but they can also be the source of embarrassing errors. For example, if a client asks for some specialized information and the e-mailer edits a portion of the usual e-mail template, the edits may cause unanticipated problems. These might include typographical errors, an awkward redundancy in content or word choice, or even an outright conflict of information if the sender forgets to make corresponding changes in another, related section.

In some cases it may be easier and safer to compose a message from scratch.

7.9 **Urgent E-Mail**

Depending on the e-mail software being used, an e-mailer may be able to indicate to the reader that a message is of high priority by marking it with a red exclamation point or other urgent-looking symbol. This feature tends to be abused by senders whose idea of a high priority doesn't necessarily correspond to their readers'. Unless you are absolutely certain that the situation is urgent, don't mark an e-mail as high-priority—particularly if it is going to someone you work for.

Even when it is urgent, you have alternatives to the red exclamation point. For example, you can send a regular (i.e., not high-priority) e-mail and then follow up with a call.

7.10 **Read Receipts**

A read receipt, which notifies the sender when his or her message has been opened or read, is another frequently abused technological tool. Use these receipts only if absolutely necessary. Many readers find them intrusive, though they will be much more receptive to a read receipt if a message is critical for business or legal reasons. Otherwise, people don't necessarily like having someone know when they have read an e-mail; they may consider the management of their e-mail correspondence to be a private matter.

7.11 **Meeting Etiquette**

The fact that it is technologically possible to check e-mail from just about anywhere doesn't mean that one *should* check e-mail from just about anywhere. The broad accessibility of e-mail through portable electronic devices is creating an epidemic of e-mail etiquette violations. It is generally impolite to check e-mail in the middle of a meeting while someone else is speaking. It can also be counter-productive. Imagine a room full of people ignoring the speaker while e-mailing under the table. Or perhaps you don't have to imagine it; perhaps you've been there.

Naturally, you have to navigate your corporate culture, the demands and expectations of your manager, and so on. But many people have no such excuse for their bad behavior. They spend meetings e-mailing other people who are not at the meeting, not because they have to but because they can. People who are actually at the meeting, of course, know what the e-mailers are doing under the table. The e-mailers risk offending not only the speaker but also others who are participating fully and thoughtfully in the discussion.

Chapter 8

Reducing E-Mail Volume

What percentage of the e-mail you receive each day at work is actually useful? For many professionals, that percentage is far lower than they would like.

No one likes spam, but spammers are not the only ones responsible for time-wasting e-mail messages. For example, businesspeople often complain that many of the messages received from their own co-workers simply aren't necessary. One strange phenomenon: far more people complain about receiving too many messages from their colleagues than admit to sending too many — but all that e-mail has to be coming from somewhere!

The focus of this chapter is on ways to reduce e-mail volume. Given the extent of the problem, the task may seem daunting, but it is nonetheless worth undertaking. At the very least, people will appreciate that you are not among those who cavalierly waste others' time with annoying and unproductive communications. Below is a list of e-mail reduction strategies.

1. Use the phone more. Or even walk over to your colleague's desk from time to time!

Don't hide behind e-mail. Despite the old adage, talk is not cheap. As discussed in Chapter 6, talking can be an important way to cultivate and maintain business relationships.

2. Don't use "Reply All" unless it is necessary.

If "Reply" suffices, it is almost always preferable to "Reply All." Imagine that you are one of ten recipients on an e-mail message. If you respond by clicking "Reply All," the sender and the other nine original recipients will all receive your message. That means you are sending not one e-mail message, but ten.

If everyone needs to see your response, then "Reply All" is fine. If only the original sender needs to see it, though, don't impose your response unnecessarily on nine extra people.

Now suppose a subset of the original group needs your response — perhaps the original sender plus three of the original recipients. In that case, you could click "Reply All" but then delete the other people's addresses from the *To* field before sending.

3. Copy only people who need to be copied.

Many professionals copy too many people on too many e-mails. Don't fall into the trap of using e-mail as a means of creating a long and many-layered electronic paper trail. True, if Joe copies everyone on everything, no one will be able to complain that he didn't inform them of a particular event or detail. They could, however, complain that he is constantly wasting their time and irritating them with unnecessary e-mails.

While it is critical to copy people, particularly one's managers, on e-mails containing information they need, it is also critical not to encroach on other people's valuable time without justification. It may be a cliché, but it's true: time is money.

Be more discriminating than the fictitious but unfortunately all too typical Joe.

4. Forward only what needs to be forwarded.

Don't forward an e-mail message to someone without thinking first about whether the message will be useful to that person.

Even if you think an e-mailed joke is hysterically funny, avoid forwarding it, or similar types of messages, to others at work. Your colleagues may not tell you if they find such messages annoying, and it is contrary to the spirit, and probably the letter, of many companies' policies on e-mail use at work.

In addition, it is not particularly efficient to forward a dialogue several pages long to an employee with a quick note at the top saying, "What do you think?" It is an extremely bad idea to send something similar to your manager, who is interested in having you save him or her time, not consume it. It is common for people to forward messages when they should instead be composing an original message that synthesizes only the issue or issues they care about.

For a discussion of some additional forwarding issues, see Section 7.4.

Chapter 9
Reader
Responsibilities

E-MAIL ETIQUETTE INVOLVES NOT ONLY THE WRITER, but also the reader. Unfortunately, an e-mail deluge has frustrated many readers and made them, on average, perhaps somewhat more impatient with the demands of e-mail management than they might have been in the early days of these electronic communications.

Despite the annoyances of e-mail, people who use it for work must be vigilant about their handling of incoming messages. Keep in mind the following guidelines.

1. Don't file or delete messages carelessly.

If you arrive at the office in the morning and encounter a hundred e-mail messages, it is natural to want to take care of them efficiently. Don't, however, file and delete so quickly that you make mistakes. Go slowly enough that you can avoid misfilings and accidental deletions.

2. Address *all* of the sender's questions or concerns.

Unfortunately, many people do not read their incoming messages with care. It is all too common, even with very clear messages consisting of no more than a couple of sentences, for the recipient to disregard the second sentence and respond only to the contents of the first. The result is that the original e-mailer must send a follow-up e-mail. If ultimately four messages are necessary instead of two, the original recipient is responsible not only for wasting the time of the e-mail sender, but also for causing annoyance.

The moral: skimming a message, or reading only the first line or two, is inadequate.

3. Don't allow too many unanswered messages to accumulate in your inbox.

If your e-mail inbox is constantly overflowing, at some point you are likely to overlook an important or time-sensitive communication. To reduce this likelihood, develop a routine that will help you keep your e-mail inbox organized.

4. Respond efficiently to important e-mail messages.

If you receive an urgent e-mail that requires a prompt response—say within a day—consider answering right away to acknowledge that you have received the e-mail and are working on a response. That may reassure an eager client or concerned manager. You might also want to indicate when you expect to send the response. It can be helpful to mark a reminder on your calendar or set an alert so that you remember to follow through by the deadline.

If for some reason you can't or don't respond to an important message quickly enough (and how quickly is quickly enough will depend on the context), apologize for the delay.

5. If a client complains that e-mails are being rejected by your company's e-mail system, do what you can to help resolve the issue.

Some companies have overeager spam filters that inexplicably reject even important and necessary e-mail messages. It is bad business to reject e-mails from clients or from others outside your firm who may be providing you with services and information you need. It can be maddening to the sender of the rejected e-mail, even more so if the recipient (you) is cavalier about the problem. Although you may have nothing to do with the problem, you are the face of your company for this person and should therefore follow up vigilantly, or have one of your employees follow up vigilantly, with your IT department or whoever is responsible for resolving the issue.

6. Don't allow e-mail to take over your working life to the detriment of other responsibilities.

Answering e-mail is probably not your only re-sponsibility at work. Some people seem to forget that, abandoning other tasks in their zeal to answer e-mail messages as soon as they show up on their computer screens. Efficiency is important, but is it actually efficient to constantly interrupt what one is doing in order to answer an e-mail the moment it arrives?

If you are a compulsive e-mail checker — and if compulsively checking e-mail is not your actual job! — consider whether you might be able to cut back on the frequency with which you check your inbox. Depending on the nature of your work, you may not be able to do so, but if you can, you may find your way to a less scattered, more productive work day.

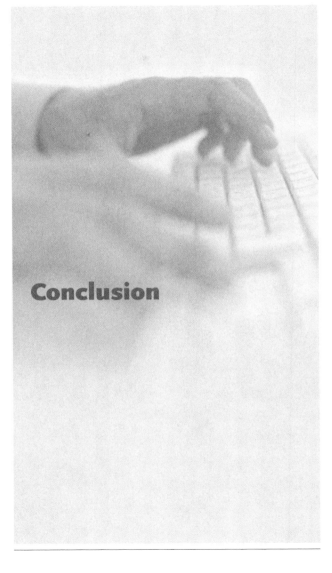

Conclusion

In the 1990s, e-mail very quickly changed the way people communicated with one another. It is not surprising that some of the social and cultural protocols surrounding e-mail use are still evolving, as such developments tend to lag behind the technological innovations that inspire them.

Unlike memos and business letters, which have historically been associated with a certain amount of professional decorum, e-mail continues to enjoy widespread use as a personal tool to connect e-mailers with family and friends. Many users of electronic mail become accustomed to a casual, intimate style and have difficulty switching to a more professional mode of communication.

For work-related e-mail, the best approach is in some ways a look to the past: treat your e-mail with the same care you would give a printed, mailed letter or a companywide memo. Especially for important messages, consider your structure carefully, revise thoroughly, print, proofread, reread, and, if necessary, revise, print, and review again.

In addition, think twice before taking advantage of the technological innovations afforded by e-mail. For example, if you are contemplating copying someone on a message, consider whether you would still copy that person if doing so required a trip to the copy machine, an envelope, and a stamp.

By applying old-fashioned attentiveness to modern technological tools, you should be well equipped to realize the full power of electronic communications in the twenty-first century.

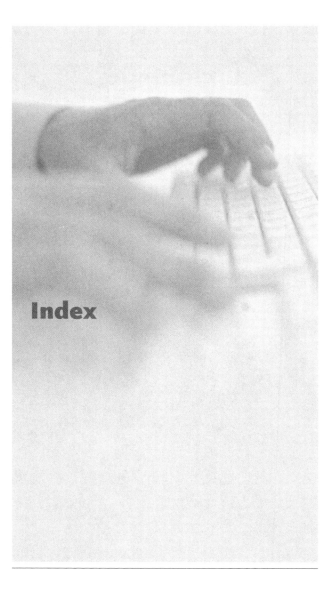

Index

abbreviations, 30–31, 40–41
active voice, 66–69
aggressive punctuation, 37, 39–40
articles, missing, 72–74
attachments, 13, 51–53, 56–57, 71–72, 102
audience, 36, 60, 61, 87, 95, 96. *See also* reader, awareness of
automatic replies, 19, 87–92

Bcc field, 92–94
because, beginning a sentence with, 62–63
Blackberrys. *See* PDAs
blind copying, 92–94
body
    of a document, 15, 45, 48–51
    of an e-mail, 11, 14–33, 102
boss, e-mailing your. *See* manager, e-mailing your
bulleting, 55–56
business correspondence,

types of, 5–7
business letters, 1, 5–6, 15, 16, 59, 121
    e-mail as substitute for, 5–6

capitalization, 13–14, 32, 35–36
Cc field, 92–93. *See also* copying
clauses, independent, 63
clichés, 74
clients, e-mailing, 5–6, 15, 16, 17, 24–25, 26, 32, 36, 82, 83, 89, 99–100, 101, 102, 105, 116–117
closings, 11, 23–27, 47
color, 30, 33
comma splices, 63
commands, 83–85
commas, 18, 36, 63
conciseness, 13, 46, 67, 72, 75
conclusions, 45, 48, 49, 57
confidential information, 96
contact information. *See*

signature files
conversation
  e-mail as substitute for, 1,
    6–7, 81–82
  value of, 81–82, 85, 110
copying, 1, 92–94, 110–111, 122
corporate culture, e-mail
  and, 2, 15, 17, 18, 20, 73, 106

dashes, 37, 38–39
development, 50, 54–55
dialogues, e-mail, 15–16, 29,
  85, 94, 96, 101, 112
direct objects, missing, 72–74

editing, 30, 35, 40, 57,
  59–79, 97, 105. *See also*
  revising
efficiency, 2, 53, 59, 61, 79,
  81, 82, 83, 96, 101, 112,
  116–117, 118
ellipses, 37, 38
e-mail volume, ways to reduce, 92, 109–112
emoticons, 40–41
employees, e-mailing your,
  83, 112
ethical issues, in e-mail, 1–2,
  94, 95–97
exclamation points, 37,
  39–40, 105

filing e-mail, 115
font, 25, 30, 33

format, e-mail, 11–33, 48–49,
  55–57, 89, 103, 104
forwarding, 1, 94–100, 111–112
From field, 6, 12, 32

gender, 19, 21, 22
grammar, 59, 64, 72–73, 76,
  89, 103. *See also* capitalization; comma splices;
  editing techniques; punctuation
greetings. *See* salutations

handheld devices. *See* PDAs
HTML, 2

imperative, 83–85
inbox, managing your, 116, 118
indenting, 23
independent clauses, 63
initials, 12, 21–22, 26
introductions, 45, 46, 48,
  49, 50, 51

jokes, forwarding, 111

length, e-mail, 22–23, 45–46,
  49, 51, 56–57, 72, 96
letters. *See* business letters
listservs, 91–92
long e-mails, 23, 45, 49–51,
  53, 56–57, 82, 96, 101, 112
lower-case letters. *See* capitalization

mailing lists, 91–92, 93–94
main idea
    of an e-mail, 45–48
    of a paragraph, 48, 54–55
managers, e-mailing your,
    15–16, 17, 19–20, 36,
    41–42, 51–53, 82, 83–85,
    96–97, 101, 105, 111, 112,
    116–117
managing relationships,
    81–85, 110
marketing, e-mail, 2, 33
meeting etiquette, 106–107
memos, 1, 5–6, 20, 45,
    56–57, 59, 121
    e-mail as substitute for, 6
message content, 11, 22–23,
    36
missing words, 38, 72–74,
    76
Mr. and *Ms.*, using in saluta-
    tions, 22
multiple recipients, address-
    ing, 15, 18–21, 92

names
    in closings, 23–27
    in *From* field, 12
    initials, 12, 21–22, 26
    recipient, 12, 15–18, 20,
        21–22, 23, 36, 48, 83
    in salutations, 21–22
    sender, 12, 23–27
    in *To* field, 12, 92

natural language, 70–72
nonverbal cues, 7–8

order of ideas, 49–53
organization, e-mail, 1, 23,
    45–57, 59, 97
ornate language, 70–72

Palms. *See* PDAs
paper trail, 111
paragraphing, 23, 48–49
passive voice, 64–69
past participles, 64, 65, 66
PDAs (personal digital as-
    sistants), 23, 73, 103–104,
    106–107
PDFs, 57
periods, 25, 36, 63
personal content, 96, 98–99
personal e-mail, 2, 38, 41, 121
plain text, 2
proofreading, 30, 59, 76, 77,
    103, 104–105, 121. *See also*
    editing
proper nouns, 13–14, 35
punctuation, 1, 30, 32, 35,
    36–40, 63, 103
    aggressive, 37, 39–40
    in closings, 25
    commas, 18, 36, 63
    dashes, 37, 38–39
    ellipses, 37, 38
    exclamation points, 37,
        39–40

periods, 25, 36, 63
question marks, 39–40
in salutations, 17, 18
semicolons, 36, 62
purpose, stating your, 1,
    45–48, 102

question marks, 39–40
quotations, favorite, 32–33

read receipts, 106
reader
    awareness of, 35, 36,
        47–49, 50, 53, 54, 66,
        70, 72, 74, 75, 76–77,
        106. *See also* audience
    responsibilities, 115–118
reading aloud, 60, 76
recipient names, 12, 15–18,
    20, 21–22, 23, 36, 48, 83
recipients
    multiple, 15, 18–21, 92, 93
    single, 15–18
relationship management,
    81–85, 110
"Reply All" function, 94, 110
replying to e-mail, 41–42,
    102, 103–104, 110, 115–118
revising, 46, 59, 121. *See also*
    editing

salutations (greetings), 11, 14,
    15–21, 22, 23, 47, 90, 92
    for multiple recipients,
        15, 18–21
    omitting, 15–16, 20, 90,
        101, 104
    for a single recipient, 15–18
sayings, favorite, 32–33
semicolons, 36, 62
sender name, 12, 23–27
sensitive subjects, commu-
    nicating about, 85, 95–97
sentence
    structure, 59, 60–69, 76
    variety, 60–63
short e-mails, 22–23, 45, 46,
    49, 51, 72, 73
signature files, 11, 14, 24, 25,
    27–33, 74–75, 89, 90, 103,
    104
    internal, 28–29
    omitting, 29, 101, 104
sincerity, 75
spacing, 23, 24, 32, 48, 104
spam, 109
    filters, 117
spell-checkers, 40, 76–77
spelling, 21, 32, 40, 76–77,
    83, 88, 89
subject lines, 6, 13–14,
    46–47, 53, 90, 101

telephone numbers, in sig-
    nature files, 29–30, 31–32,
    89, 90
templates, e-mail, 104–105
thank-you e-mails, 26–27

time management, e-mail
    and, 117–118
To field, 6, 12, 15, 77, 92, 94,
    110
tone, 7–8, 89, 90–91
trite language, 74–75
typographical errors, 32, 77,
    88, 105

unsolicited e-mail, 29, 89
urgent e-mail, 39–40,
    82–83, 105, 116–117

vague language, 69–70
viruses, 102
volume. *See* e-mail volume,
    ways to reduce

warmth, 15, 56
word choice, 57, 59, 69–75,
    105
wordiness, 13, 63, 70–72,
    74–75